P9-AQT-035
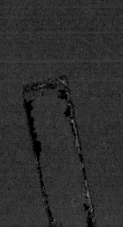

FISHING
FOR BEGINNERS

Fishing

EDITED BY PETE CORNACCHIA

JOHN FABIAN

for Beginners

NEW YORK   1974   ATHENEUM

Photographs by John Fabian, Pete Cornacchia, and Steve Winitzky
Diagrams by Steve Cornacchia
COPYRIGHT © 1974 BY JOHN FABIAN
ALL RIGHTS RESERVED
LIBRARY OF CONGRESS CATALOG CARD NUMBER 74-77842
ISBN 0-689-10614-9
PUBLISHED SIMULTANEOUSLY IN CANADA BY MCCLELLAND & STEWART LTD.
MANUFACTURED IN THE UNITED STATES OF AMERICA BY
COMPOSITION BY NEWTYPE INC., WALLINGTON, NEW JERSEY
PRINTED AND BOUND BY HALLIDAY LITHOGRAPH CORPORATION,
HANOVER, MASSACHUSETTS
DESIGNED BY KATHLEEN CAREY
FIRST EDITION

IN DEDICATION TO

LORI, JOHNNY, SCOTT AND BRIAN

Contents

FISHING
FOR BEGINNERS

The Making of
a Fisherman

THE WATER WAS so clear that I could easily see the five salmon eggs scattered on the sand bottom twenty feet below the surface. Peering over the edge of the wharf, I could follow my line down to the sinker. But I could not see the two feet of transparent leader. When I gave a gentle tug on the line, however, one of the pink eggs moved. I knew my hook was in that one.

It seemed like hours before a rainbow trout swam slowly from under the piling, picked up one of the eggs and swallowed it. Nosing around on the bottom, the fish ate three more after a careful look at each one. The only egg left was the one on my hook! The trout swam around it, looked it over and turned away. As the fish began to move off, my trembling fingers accidentally pulled the line. The egg twitched and the trout grabbed it.

For a second, I was too surprised to do anything. Then I yanked on the line and felt the tug of a ten-inch fish that must have been just as surprised. He tugged, pulled and flopped violently as, hand over hand, I brought him to the surface and lifted him onto the pier.

The fat rainbow, with gleaming pink sides and greenish back, was my first trout. My mother remembers the occasion much better than I do, for I was only four; until then I had caught nothing other than goldfish with doughballs in our backyard lily pond.

Since then, I have devoted a large part of my life to learning about fish and trying to catch them.

Fishing tackle and methods have changed through the years, but your chances of catching fish are as good as mine were then. Probably better, for gear and methods have been refined and the agencies responsible for maintaining fish in our lakes, streams and salt water have given anglers good returns on the money paid in license fees. If fishing weren't as rewarding and enjoyable as ever, we wouldn't have over 75 million people dangling hook and line at least once a year. So you won't be alone on the bank or in a boat. You'll have plenty of company.

On some of the more popular waters, of course, you may have to wait your turn for a rock or a spot on the bank. For all the people who will be trying to catch something, there will usually be enough fish to go around. Yet a few fishermen will be doing most of the catching. It's true that about one of every ten anglers will stand out with a better catch than the other nine combined. Why?

It's seldom luck alone, for usually it will be the same fisherman who ends up with the good catch. I'll give you odds that if you study him, you'll find that he—or she—knows his tackle and how to use it better than the others. He may not always be the best caster of the group, but he will be better than most. You'll find, too, that he has studied the fish and the water he's fishing. Not just by reading books, either, though he probably could write one. As much as a human being can, he has learned to think like a fish. He wasn't born with this faculty, and it didn't come to him in one day. He fished a lot and he used his head as well as his tackle.

I know this fisherman. I know how he cares for that tackle, how he treats his catch and his fellow fishermen. He is prepared and ready to fish before he leaves home.

Too many anglers seem to think, "If I get my hook in the water, my chances are just as good as the next guy's." They're kidding themselves. Luck plays a small part. The lucky fisherman may not realize it, but he's the unlucky one. When you or I catch a fish without realizing how or why, we've missed the challenge of outwitting that fish and the satisfaction of knowing that we can go about it in the same manner again and catch another one.

Learning—that's what fishing is all about and why it's fun. If you're still trying to learn something on every trip twenty years from now, you will be the

5

fisherman who is catching more than the others.

A professional ballplayer or golfer knows that it takes more than natural ability to stay at the top for long. He knows that he must keep working hard and developing his skills to make the utmost of his natural ability. The good golfer knows he must eat, sleep and live his game if he is to be better than most of us.

You can become an excellent fisherman if you approach the sport with that attitude. And, in contrast to beginners in many sports, you are never too young or too old to start.

Like golf, fishing can be terribly frustrating, particularly at the beginning. Extremely important in becoming a good angler is to get started the easiest way, with the least complication.

Reading this book will help you get on your way. But remember, no amount of written material, conversation, film or photos alone can teach you all there is to know about fishing. I've read many books on fishing and I still read just about everything that I can find on the subject. But if you are to become a good fisherman, which you can, you will find that more fish are caught in water than in books.

I will try here to give you a straight and honest introduction to angling for the fish in that water. After we've gone over basic equipment and how to use it, along with some basic methods and ideas that helped my children and other beginners to get started, we'll go out and meet the fish where they live.

Fishing Tackle

IN THE SIMPLEST form of angling man would reach into the water and catch fish barehanded. This form of fishing is still a way of life in some parts of the world. But civilized man, seeking fish not only for food but recreation, has found that fishing is all the more enjoyable when he uses equipment and abides by rules that give his quarry a sporting chance.

I happen to get the most enjoyment from fishing with a fly rod. Fly casting in itself offers a challenge and a great deal of personal satisfaction. I've found, though, that I cannot limit myself to fly fishing. In my tackle room is a great variety of rods, reels and lines designed for specific types of water or fish.

There are many ways of taking fish, of course, but most of us rely on one of four basic methods—fly

Different kinds of tackle, top to bottom: fly casting, bait casting, spinning and trolling

casting, spin casting, bait casting or trolling. And for each method, there is a particular type of tackle which is most suitable.

While man has yet to come up with a fishing outfit that's ideal for all waters, we can settle for one that will handle almost anything from panfish to salmon with reasonable efficiency. It will serve you on streams, rivers, ponds and lakes. A heavier model of this same outfit will satisfy most ocean requirements.

This outfit will adjust to fishing in spring, summer, fall and winter. It's the only choice for the majority of beginning fishermen. I'm talking about a spinning out-fit.

If you must limit yourself to a single rig to handle a variety of fishing, go with a medium-sized spinning outfit and a carefully planned tackle box. You will learn faster and catch more fish. Later, you will have less trouble mastering the art of fly casting or bait casting because you will already know how to catch fish and you will be able to concentrate on the casting alone.

In casting with a spinning outfit, the line is uncoiled from a fixed spool by the pull of your bait or lure as it travels through the air. Unlike the spool on a level-wind reel, the drum on a spinning reel does not rotate. It works something like pulling coils of string straight off the end of a stick. You'll find that with a spinning outfit you will seldom have any trouble with backlashes and will be able to make long casts with even the lightest baits and lures. You'll learn to make those long casts in

9

A rainbow trout. Big fish or small fish, the best all-around outfit is a spinning outfit.

This young lady used a salt-water spinning outfit and a surface plug to land this striped bass.

a fraction of the time required with other types of outfits. And spinning outfits are less expensive than the others.

You have a choice of two types of spinning reels. One, called closed-face, has a conical hood covering the spool and the revolving pickup bail which recoils your line on the retrieve. Closed-face reels are mounted on top of the rod handle, and the cast is controlled by the thumb on a pushbutton. The open-face reel favored by a great majority of anglers does not have a hood. It mounts on the underside of the rod, and the cast is controlled by the index finger.

Along with a great many others, I prefer the open-face reel for several reasons. Without the hood, I can always see the amount and condition of line on the spool. The occasional snarl can be untangled more quickly and easily. I can make longer casts and have the flexibility for quick changes of spools holding different sizes of line.

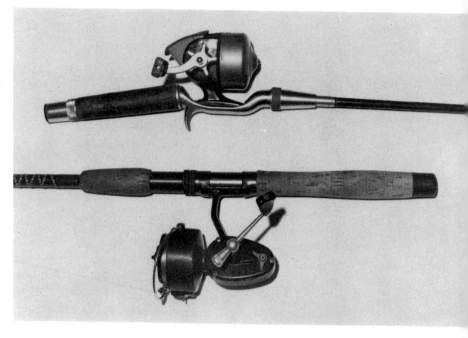

Top: closed-face spinning casting reel. Bottom: the open-face spinning reel.

Choosing an
All-Round Outfit

WHEN YOU BUY fishing tackle you get what you pay for as you do with almost anything you buy. Usually—not always, though—the more that you spend on a rod or reel, the more you will get in durability and service. That's not to say it won't pay you to shop around. You may find the item you want on sale at a price well below the going rate elsewhere in town. But always try to buy the best equipment that you can afford.

And what's the best? Well, let's take a look at what I feel is the best all-round spinning outfit.

The reel is an open-face model of medium size, with frame and stem made of steel. When you buy one, be sure that the spool is easily removable so that you will be able to replace it quickly with another holding lighter or heavier line. An extra spool will come with most

A medium-sized spinning outfit will serve you well on almost any water.

reels of medium quality or better, and you may want to buy more spools later. Make sure, too, that the reel has a dependable drag device that can be adjusted to the strength of your line. As for brands, my favorites are Garcia's Mitchell 00 and the Quick-Finessa 220. Both are guaranteed, and spare parts are usually stocked by dealers.

For handling small- and medium-size fish, a two-piece fiberglass rod 6½ feet long and with medium action will do a fine job. For bigger fish, go to 7 feet. Line guides should be large enough that your line on a cast won't be "choked" as it comes off the reel in spirals. The fixed reel seat should be set in a cork handle, and the rod should have a sturdy case for carrying. My top choice is a Fenwick FS65, which weighs 4⅞ ounces and will handle lures of ¼ to ⅝ ounce on 4- to 12-pound test line.

The most suitable line for spinning is nylon monofilament. A light lure will not cast well on a heavy line and neither will a heavy lure on a light line, so you will need different sizes of line. You will find that on the rod and reel we're talking about, 6-pound and 10-pound test will do quite well at the start. Later you may want to go to lighter or heavier line. It's less expensive to buy line on bulk rolls of 200 yards or more. Buy 200 yards of 6-pound and 300 yards of 10-pound.

Nylon monofilament line is tough and supple but will become brittle and weak with use. The first 100 feet on your spool should be checked frequently for frayed

15

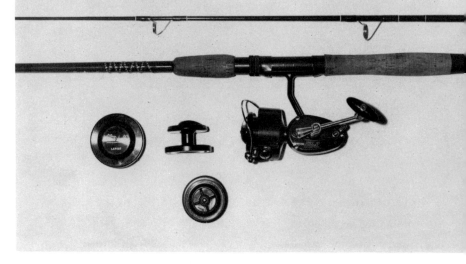

Two-piece fiberglass rod and spinning reel with extra spools

Limp monofilament line, small capacity spool, large capacity spool and casting weight with snap swivel

spots whenever you're fishing. Extra spools or rolls of line should be stored out of the sunlight when not in use.

Monofilament comes in various colors; most anglers, for their own reasons, have their favorite colors. I like a light blue-gray or neutral hue.

When you're learning how to cast, the softness or limpness of your line is much more important than the color. The stiffer your line, the more problems you will encounter in casting.

So go out and shop around. If you're planning to be trying primarily for bigger fish, twenty pounds or more, get salt-water models with the same features we've discussed and heavier line in 15-pound to 20-pound test. Whatever you choose, ask the dealer to assemble the outfit and show you how to use it. Most dealers will be happy to do this.

And while you're getting it all together, pick up some No. 8 snap swivels and a ¼-ounce rubber weight for casting practice.

Learning Spinning

WELL, IT LOOKS as if you've found a good all-round spinning outfit, all right. You take good care of it, and it should give you many years of enjoyment. If you heed what it says about care and cleaning in the manual that came with the reel, you won't need to buy another one for a long time. Treat that rod right and it will do all that you ask of it.

Now, let's go outside and see what this outfit will do. But first, let's go through the instruction pamphlets. Be sure to fill out the guarantee form and mail it to the manufacturers right away so they will have ready reference should you need repairs or replacement.

You don't need to know all the parts of the spinning reel, but the pickup bail, the crank handle and the drag adjustment knob all have important functions, and you

18

should learn what each of them does. As you go through the instructions on operating the reel, step by step, play with it until you know how to open the bail with your fingers, close it by turning the handle, tighten or loosen the drag, and remove and replace the spool.

Let's not put the two sections of the rod together until we get outside, where we won't have to worry about bumping furniture. Mom wouldn't care to learn that the crash she heard was her vase hitting the floor, any more than you would like suddenly to have a three-piece rod.

But it's easier to handle the reel when it's fastened to the butt section of the rod, so let's do that now. Screw those rings down good and tight.

Now, let's put some line on those spools. Most sporting goods stores will fill them for you from bulk rolls if you wish, or you can buy your line on spools of 100 to 300 yards, as you have done.

We may as well start with the small spool; it has less line capacity because of the thicker drum, but it will hold about 175 yards of 6-pound test line. The large capacity spool will hold about 250 yards of 10-pound test.

First, tie a slip loop in the end of your line. Any type of knot will do, just so the loop is large enough to slip over the rim of the spool and will draw tight against the drum when you pull on the line. Check pages 39–40 if you're a little shaky on knots.

Pull the loop through the big bottom guide on the rod, the first one above the reel. Open the pickup bail and place the slip loop over the rim of the spool, then draw the loop tight on the drum. When you turn the reel handle, the bail will close and pick up your line. Now you're ready to fill the spool, which is all the easier to do when someone is holding the roll of line for you. The side of the roll should be facing the spool.

The line must uncoil from the end of the roll and should be cranked onto the reel spool under moderate tension. You can do this by using one hand to press the line against the guide while you turn the reel handle with the other. After winding about ten or twelve feet of line onto the spool, allow some slack in the line. If it's twisting, turn the roll so that the line will come off the other side.

Most people will put either too much or too little line on the spool. Too little line will cut down your casting distance. Too much will result in several coils leaving the spool at once, creating a nasty snarl.

When your spool is filled properly, about ⅛ inch of the spool lip will be showing above the line. Place a wide rubber band around the line so it won't come off the spool.

So let's fill the other spool. And now, let's go outside. By outside, I mean some place where you'll have plenty of room for casting and won't be tangling with shrubs, fences or whatever. Most front or back yards will do for practice, but if you don't have one, a park, playground or school yard will be fine. You don't need

The line must come off one end of the bulk spool to avoid twisting as it is wound into the reel spool.

Filled properly, the line will come to about 1/8 of an inch from the front lip of the spool.

water to practice casting, but beware of power lines and try to pick a place without many trees. If you go to a park or an empty lot, try to go at a time when not many people are around.

Now we can assemble the rod. The tip section fits onto the butt section by means of a ferrule. The two parts should be pushed together firmly by twisting lightly while the guides are kept in a straight line.

In most cases, the lighter the line the easier it is to handle. So let's start with the 6-pound. To string line through the guides, we can release it from the spool either by opening the bail or loosening the drag and pulling it off. But when the bail is open, too much of the free line may come off at once. For now, loosen the drag and pull the line off as it's needed.

String the line through each guide, making sure that it goes through the center hole, *not* between the holding bracket and the rod.

When you have the line through the top guide, pull another six feet off the spool. Tie one of those snap swivels to the line, then snap the ¼-ounce rubber casting weight to the swivel.

Learning to cast with a spinning outfit requires very little explanation. It comes almost naturally and usually can be mastered in a few minutes. For most beginners, the greatest difficulty comes in timing when to release the line as the rod is brought forward.

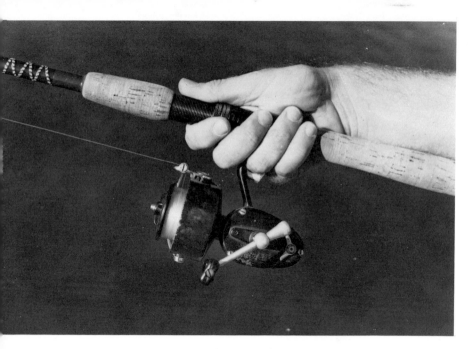

The grip is firm but comfortable. The rod points ahead.

The index finger picks up the line and the other hand opens the bail.

The wrist is used to bring the rod back smoothly but sharply to a vertical position. Pause slightly . . .

. . . and bring the rod forward and release the line. Timing the release is critical for accuracy and distance.

As the cast ends, touch the spool lip with the index finger to stop extra coils from coming off the spool.

When the handle is turned, the bail closes, picks up the line and wraps it on the spool as you retrieve.

Without tension on the line, it will wrap loosely on the spool.

Loose line on the spool results in too many coils coming off at once. On the next cast, your snarl may look like this.

Hold the rod straight out in front of you, pointing in the direction of your cast. Reel the line in until the weight is about eight inches from the tip of the rod. The hand holding the rod should encircle the reel seat, with the reel stem extending downward between the middle and fourth fingers. Thumb should be on top of the cork handle. This is the grip for casting. It should be firm but comfortable.

With your index finger, pick up the line in front of the bail. Just hold it lightly in the crook of your finger so that it will not spill out as you open the bail with the other hand. Your index finger is holding the line, the bail is open, the rubber weight is dangling about eight inches below the tip of the rod and you're ready to cast.

Pick out a spot in front of you, about fifty feet away. Point the rod at your target, then start the cast by bringing the rod back smoothly but sharply to a vertical position. Use your wrist more than your elbow or shoulder. The rod is stopped when it's pointed almost straight up, but the casting weight continues backward over your shoulder, bending the rod rearward. When you feel the casting weight at or near the end of its thrust, bring the rod forward in a crisp downstroke and release the line by straightening your index finger.

Whoops, the weight went straight up and didn't get near the target. The line was released a little too soon. Reel up until the weight is within eight inches of the top, and try it again. You let go too late that time,

The overhead cast: Aim at the target, rod out front, weight about eight inches from the tip.

Bring the rod back toward your shoulder, using your wrist. Stop when the rod is almost vertical.

Your wrist stopped as the rod was vertical, but the motion of the weight continues to bend the rod backward. Now the rod is ready to catapult the casting weight forward toward the target.

The wrist brings the rod forward and downward. Release the line now to let the weight go out.

Touch your index finger to the lip of the spool as the weight hits the target, to keep extra coils from coming off.

which is why the weight slammed straight to the ground. Try again. There, your weight almost made it to the target! Keep trying now, until you feel that your timing is right and you're hitting close to your spot more often than not. It will take a while before you really get the feel of it, but it's better to learn now so you won't be wasting your time when we go fishing.

At the end of each cast, touch the spool with your index finger to stop extra coils of line from coming off the spool. Slack coils will tangle on a spinning reel. If you don't have tension on the line when you start to reel in, the line will wrap on the spool loosely and the next cast will pull several coils off at once. That will be your first snarl. As you continue to practice casting, always finish each cast by touching the spool rim. Catch the line with your index finger immediately and lift the rod tip to take up all the slack in the line before you start to retrieve. Once you get in the habit of doing this, the line will wrap tightly after every cast.

The first cast you've learned is the standard overhead cast, the one you will use in most of your fishing. Trees, branches and other obstructions behind or in front of you may require a different cast. It's a good idea to learn the sidearm and backhand casts while you're still practicing. Once you get the timing of the release on the overhead cast, the others will be easy.

If you have small hands and the rod feels overly heavy, go to the two-handed cast. It's done the same as the overhead except that the other hand grips the lower

The sidearm cast: The rod swings to the side.

The two-handed cast gets distance. Note that the weight hangs about two feet from the tip.

The bow and arrow cast: The rod is bent by holding the weight in your hand and releasing the weight and line at almost the same time. This cast is not used often in fishing. Watch out for hooks if you try this cast with a lure.

The backhand cast is handy when trees or foliage make a regular cast impossible. Similar to the overhead cast except the rod comes back over the other shoulder.

part of the rod handle. You may feel more comfortable if you bring the rod back slightly to the side.

Whichever type of cast seems best for you, keep practicing until you're consistently able to drop the weight reasonably close to the target area on short casts of twenty to sixty feet.

Sooner or later you will want to see how far you can cast. On the longer casts, you will encounter wind drift. You will learn to allow for a crosswind by casting more to the left or right of the target. With the wind behind you, aim your cast high and the wind will carry it out. To overcome wind from the front, cast low over the water. Otherwise, the wind will push your lure back toward you.

You should be casting well enough to catch fish after about an hour of practice. Remember to wrap the line tightly on the spool when you retrieve, or much of your practice time will be wasted in untangling snarls caused by loose coils.

Now that you're putting the casting weight close to your mark most of the time, let's experiment a little with the drag adjustment. On your reel and most others, the drag adjustment knob is located on the face of the spool. Turn it in one direction to increase friction or drag on the spool, in another to loosen so that it will revolve more freely.

With the pickup bail closed, try to pull some line from the reel. If the drag is too tight, you will break the line. If it is too loose, the reel will give line with little

The drag adjustment knob is usually located on the front of the spool face. If the drag is set right, a fish cannot break your line.

or no resistance. The objective is to adjust the drag so that the line comes from the reel grudgingly without breaking. The lighter your line, the less drag you will need.

To get a better idea of how the drag can help you in handling a fish, tie the end of your lightest line to a tree, pole or anything stationary that has no sharp edges to cut the line. Adjust your drag so that you can pull line off the spool, but not too easily. Hold the rod up at a forty-five-degree angle. Now walk backward. That will force the line to be pulled off the spool in much the same manner as if you were playing a fish.

Walk back about forty feet, holding the rod up at the same angle. Now tighten the drag until the line cannot be pulled from the spool. Keeping the rod up, try to break the line with a steady pull. Can't do it, can you? As long as the rod is held upright, it's almost impossible to break the line with a steady pull. Though monofilament will stretch to some extent, the main reason the line does not break is that the strain is absorbed by the rod as it bends. You probably will be able to break the line by jerking sharply, but you also may break the rod. So always resist the urge to jerk hard, whether you're playing a fish or trying to free your hook from a limb or rock.

When you're unable to pull free from an object that you've hooked unintentionally and must break the line, point the rod directly at the object. Tighten the drag or hold the spool so that it won't give line, then back away. That loud bang is what you will hear if your drag is too tight when you hook a big fish.

Knots, Hooks and Terminal Rigging

SINCE THAT DAY millions of years ago when man first reached into water and caught a fish with his hand, nobody has come up with a way to attach a hook or lure to a line without tying a knot. Man did learn long before he discovered the world was round that there are many ways of tying knots, but some ways are better than others. So, unless you have something in mind to replace the knot, you will need to learn to tie those that will serve you best. And since all knots are weaker than the line itself, you will want as few as possible between you and the fish.

The slick finish of monofilament line allows common knots to slip, so I want you to learn the three knots that were developed particularly for this type of line.

DIAGRAM I   **KNOTS**

IMPROVED CLINCH KNOT
(FOR JOINING LINE TO HOOK, LURE, SWIVEL OR WEIGHT)

Double end back from eye
of hook; take five turns
around the standing line.

Thrust end between eye
and end of first loop, then
back through large loop.

Slowly pull up until tight,
and snip end off close
to knot.

BLOOD KNOT (FOR JOINING TWO LINES)

Cross the ends and twist
one side five times around
the other. Push the end
through the cross and hold.

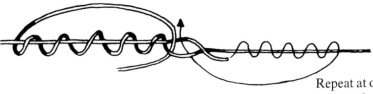

Repeat at opposite end,
twisting five times in the
same direction. Push the
end through the center lap

Slowly pull up until tight, allowing the
turns to gather neatly. Trim the ends or
leave one end long if you wish to make a dropper.

END LOOP KNOT

(FOR MAKING A LOOP IN THE END OF YOUR LINE OR LEADER)

Form a double strand six
inches long.

Fold the bend back and
spiral around the double
strand five times.

Insert the end through the
first loop and pull until
it is tight.

IMPROVED CLINCH KNOT. This knot is for tying almost anything to the end of line or leader. You will use this knot more than any other. Using about two feet of 10-pound test line, follow the steps in the diagram until you are able to tie this knot quickly and smoothly.

Insert the line through the eye of a hook, lure, swivel or casting weight. Wrap the end of the line around the main line at least five times. Insert the end between the eye and the first wrap, then between the five wraps and the loop just formed. Keeping tension on the end of the line, pull steadily on the main line and the wraps will compress into a neat and secure knot. On this or any other knot, don't try to take short cuts. You won't save that much time and you will pay dearly in loss of knot strength.

BLOOD KNOT. This is the best knot for joining two lines together. You will use it to tie a length of lighter line or leader to your main line, to mend a broken line or to add line to your spool. Practice with different sizes of line, for you will be using this knot at times to join lines of different size.

Lap the ends of the strands to be joined. Twist one end about the standing part of the opposite line, making at least five wraps or turns. Count the turns to be sure. Four turns can drop the strength of 10-pound monofilament down to 8½ pounds. Bend the end back over the turns and place it between strands. Shift your hold to prevent unwinding.

Repeat the procedure for the opposite side, winding

41

five turns in the same direction. Push the ends through the strands at the center of the lap. Pull the knot up slowly and tightly, allowing the turns to gather, and clip off the ends. Do not attempt to break them off by hand.

If you wish to make a dropper on your leader for adding another hook or weight, tie a blood knot and leave one of the ends long enough for the dropper.

IMPROVED LOOP KNOT. You may wish to use this knot in tying a loop at the end of your line for attaching lures, weights or leader.

Form a double strand by bending back about four to six inches from the end. Fold the "U" bend back and spiral it around itself five times. Insert the end of the "U" bend through the first loop made by its backward turn. Pull it up as tight as possible without breaking.

There are other useful knots, but these three will get you started. Remember, a knot is necessary. It is also the weakest part of your line, so learn to tie your knots carefully and correctly.

HOOKS

Now you're ready for hooks. There are so many different types that it would be confusing to try to mention them all. For now, we need consider only two general types—the single hooks for fishing with bait or fly and the treble hooks which are commonly used on lures and plugs.

With most hooks, you have a wide choice of size, and the size is designated by number. In most cases, the

Practice tying knots at home so you won't waste fishing time.

smaller the hook the larger the number. A No. 12, for instance, is a small hook used on flies or for offering bait to panfish. For most bait fishing, sizes 4 to 8 are the favorites. Most tackle shops will offer hooks ranging from tiny 22's to giant 12/0's. The fresh-water hooks usually have a bronze finish, while the larger salt-water hooks are nickel-plated to prevent rust.

Because of the difference in sizes of fish and methods of angling for them, there is no all-round hook. You will want to carry a variety of shapes and sizes. Lures and plugs will usually have hooks in sizes permitting the proper action, so for now we will be concerned only with hooks for fishing with bait.

The best and most popular design is the eagle claw. You can buy this hook in different sizes, either in boxes of singles or in packets of snelled hooks on short lengths of sturdy monofilament leader. Snelled hooks usually are tied to the appropriate strength of leader for the size of the hook, which eliminates some of the guesswork for beginners.

For small- to medium-size fish, I prefer hooks from 6's down to 12's. For bass, trout over four pounds, salmon, steelhead, pike and other large fish, size 6 up to No. 2 should do the job.

So-called weedless hooks have springy guards of thin wire to avoid hangups and are favorites with bass fishermen. These are preferred in sizes 4 to 2/0.

Make sure that your hooks are always sharp, particularly when you're fishing in salt water. Even the nickel-plated hooks tend to rust on the point and barb.

The bending rod absorbs most of the pressure, but terminal rigging must be tied together with good knots or you will lose the fish before he gets this close.

Use a file or honing stone.

TERMINAL TACKLE

From the end of your line down to the hook or hooks, you will use what is known as terminal rigging or tackle. This can include leader, swivels, sinkers, lures and the hooks.

LEADERS. A leader is a lighter piece of monofilament in varying lengths, depending on the situation. In many types of spin fishing a leader is not necessary. The lure or hook can be tied directly to the line.

A leader serves two purposes. Since it is of smaller diameter than the line, it is less apt to be seen by fish. Being lighter and weaker than the line, it will break first when your lure or bait is snagged hopelessly on a snag or the bottom. While you will lose your terminal rigging, the parting leader will at least save your line.

Though the leader is smaller than the line, it cannot appreciably differ in size. For instance, a 2-pound leader cannot be tied securely to 12-pound test line. A leader should not be less than half the size of the line.

SWIVELS. Because of the way that the line peels off the fixed spool of a spinning reel, it can become twisted very easily. To reduce chances of twisted line, a swivel should be used in attaching lures, bait or sinkers which rotate or revolve. Most spinning lures come with swivels attached, but I always carry a selection of snap swivels which are tied to the line and snapped to the

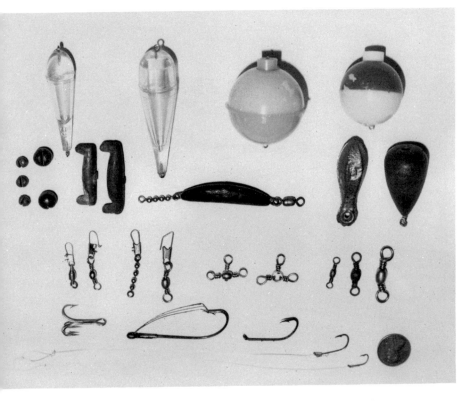

Top row: a penny, size 12 and 6 snelled hooks, a No. 2 bait hook, a No. 2/0 weedless hook and a treble hook
Second row: regular swivels, 3-way swivels and snap swivels
Third row: bottom-holding sinkers, a trolling weight with swivels, clamp-on weights and two sizes of split shot
Fourth row: round floats for still-fishing, teardrop bubbles for fly fishing

lure or sinker. I also carry regular swivels for connecting leader to line, and a three-way swivel is useful when the sinker or lure will hang from a dropper. Note uses of swivels on the diagram of different riggings.

WEIGHTS. Sinkers are used to get a lure or bait to the desired depth and as added weight for easier casting. Refrain from using more weight than is needed. Usually, smaller fish require small baits or lures and equally small sinkers. For larger fish in deeper water you will need larger weights.

In using clamp-on sinkers or split-shot, many of us often pinch them together with our teeth. But you will find that in the group with fewer cavities and nicer teeth are the fishermen who use pliers in clamping sinkers to line.

BOBBERS. At times you may want to keep your bait suspended at a certain depth and distance from shore or boat. This is easily done by attaching a small float to your line at the desired distance above the bait. A float, more commonly called a bobber, is another bit of terminal tackle that helps make your spinning outfit versatile. By using a bobber as a weight for casting, you can turn your spinning rig into a very effective fly fishing outfit.

I use two types of bobbers, one for still-fishing with bait and another for casting flies or very light natural baits such as insects.

My still-fishing bobbers are round and finished in red and white. A spring pushbutton extends a hooked wire

48

DIAGRAM II   DIFFERENT TERMINAL RIGGINGS

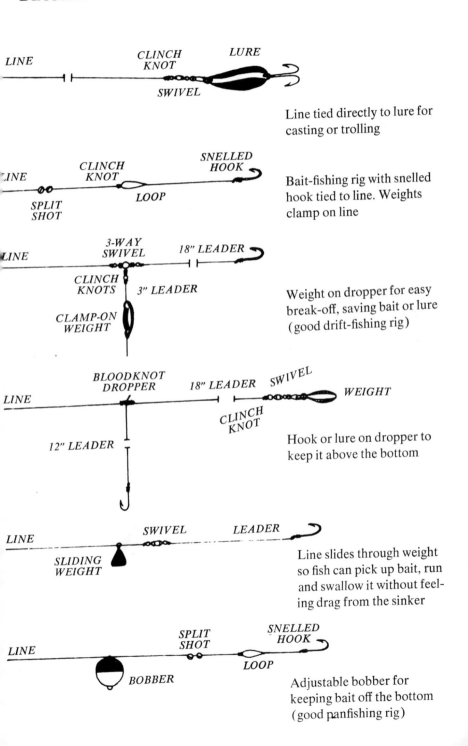

LINE — CLINCH KNOT — LURE — SWIVEL

Line tied directly to lure for casting or trolling

LINE — CLINCH KNOT — SNELLED HOOK — LOOP — SPLIT SHOT

Bait-fishing rig with snelled hook tied to line. Weights clamp on line

LINE — 3-WAY SWIVEL — 18" LEADER — CLINCH KNOTS — 3" LEADER — CLAMP-ON WEIGHT

Weight on dropper for easy break-off, saving bait or lure (good drift-fishing rig)

LINE — BLOODKNOT DROPPER — 18" LEADER — SWIVEL — CLINCH KNOT — WEIGHT — 12" LEADER

Hook or lure on dropper to keep it above the bottom

LINE — SWIVEL — LEADER — SLIDING WEIGHT

Line slides through weight so fish can pick up bait, run and swallow it without feeling drag from the sinker

LINE — SPLIT SHOT — SNELLED HOOK — LOOP — BOBBER

Adjustable bobber for keeping bait off the bottom (good panfishing rig)

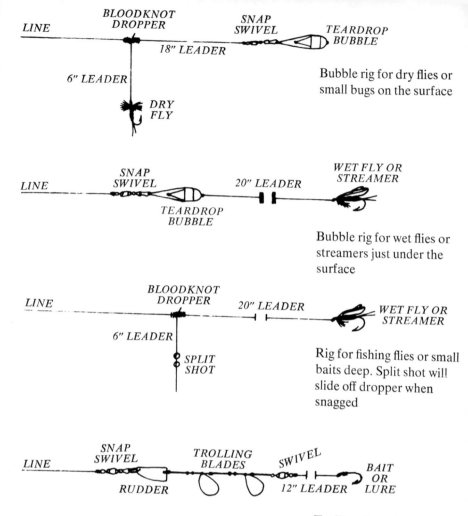

Bubble rig for dry flies or small bugs on the surface

Bubble rig for wet flies or streamers just under the surface

Rig for fishing flies or small baits deep. Split shot will slide off dropper when snagged

Trolling rig with attractor blades ahead of bait or lure

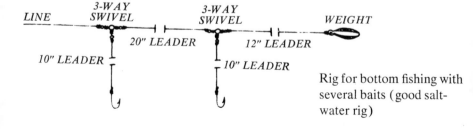

Rig for bottom fishing with several baits (good saltwater rig)

to which I attach the line simply by wrapping it around the hook two or three turns. When the button is released, the wire draws the line against the bobber. Length of line between bobber and bait can be adjusted easily, and the red-white color combination is easy to keep in sight even with a wind chop on the water.

The other bobber that I carry is made of clear plastic, a bubble shaped like a teardrop. This one has a screw eye at each end and can be used in two ways: It can be tied to the end of the line with a dropper above it, or to the line with a leader extending from the other end. Always use a snap swivel with this bobber, or it will cause your line to twist.

In selecting any of your terminal tackle, size is determined by the size of fish you will be seeking and the water conditions. In low and clear water, terminal tackle should be as small and light as possible to avoid alarming the fish. If the water is roily or high, size will be of less importance.

The following diagram shows some of the basic ways of rigging terminal tackle. Study them carefully and refer to them frequently. You will discover variations and figure out new ways of rigging to suit your situation.

Baits and Lures

LIKE ALL CREATURES, fish must have food. They eat whenever they are ready to eat and that seems to be most of the time, which is fortunate for anglers. Fish, except during their spawning period, are almost constantly searching for food. Rarely do they get so full that they will not take one more bite. They seem to have an awareness that they must stock up during the periods of plenty to tide them over the lean times.

But no matter how hungry a fish may be or how much food is available, his appetite can be dampened by changing water conditions and by caution. For all his need of nourishment, he has a stronger concern for self-preservation.

Fish may stop feeding when the water is either too warm or too cold for proper function of their bodily

These trout fell for salmon eggs drifted along the bottom.

processes, or when the water is either too low and clear or high and muddy. But when conditions are right and they are not frightened or suspicious, they can be caught at any time with the right lure or bait presented in the right way—because they're always hungry.

The surest way to catch a fish is to offer him whatever food he happens to be taking at the moment, with a hook in it. The use of natural food to catch fish is called bait fishing.

A small fish feeds mostly on tiny aquatic insects and crustaceans. As he grows, his diet expands to larger insects, any fish small enough for him to swallow and other creatures that live in the water or fall into it.

BAITS

In salt water, the bait will almost always be fish or parts of fish: anchovies, herring, shrimp, eels, squid, mussels, clams or crabs. These baits are available at tackle shops, and in some areas you may be able to catch them yourself.

Fresh-water baits are of greater variety and include some that are not natural, such as cheese, corn and marshmallows. In all fishing, the best bait to use is whatever is catching fish at that particular time and place. You will find that some waters are closed to the use of bait or certain kinds of bait. Usually, the purpose of such restrictions is to prevent overfishing or the

DIAGRAM III   **HOW TO HOOK BAIT**

Live minnows rigged for still fishing

Dead minnow rigged for casting

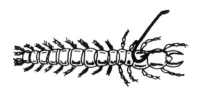

Nymph hooked under collar

Grasshopper hooked through body

Hooking a live worm

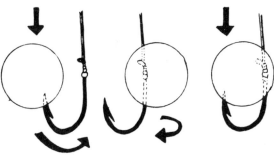

Rigging a single salmon egg

rapid spread of prolific but undesirable fishes which are brought to a stream or lake as live bait.

Now let's talk a little about the best and most commonly used baits in fresh water.

More fish are taken on worms than on any other kind of bait. I can't think of any fresh-water fish that cannot be caught on worms, from the smallest varieties to the big nightcrawlers found in lawns and gardens. In some areas you must dig for your worms with a shovel. They will usually be found in moist and rather soft dirt, so the digging will be fairly easy. You won't need a shovel if you live in an area which has nightcrawlers, giant worms up to ten inches long. A nightcrawler is a lot of worm and usually enough to make several baits for small fish.

When I want nightcrawlers, I start the water sprinklers and soak the lawn in late afternoon. Soon after dark, the worms will rise part way from their holes and stretch out on the wet grass with tail end still anchored in the hole for a quick withdrawal when approached. Searching over the lawn with a flashlight, I walk softly and slowly so that the worms will not be alarmed by ground vibrations. When I spot a nightcrawler, I ease up to it as quietly as possible and grab it firmly midway along the section extending from the hole. If I'm too slow or clumsy, the worm is gone in a lightning-quick contraction. When I make a good grab, I keep a firm grip until the anchored tail section relaxes in a few seconds, then lift the worm from the hole and place it in

56

a plastic or paper container. Damp newspaper, shredded and mixed with moist dirt, will keep worms lively for several days at least.

Finding and catching natural baits can be almost as much fun as the fishing. Along most streams, depending on the time of year, insects can be found in bushes, along the bank or in the water. A net with fine mesh is handy for catching insects which are small but still large enough to impale on a hook. Among those to be found on land are grasshoppers, crickets, caterpillars and the larger stone flies. In the water, look under rocks for crayfish, hellgrammites and other insect larvae, leeches and snails. If possible, keep these baits alive until you are ready to use them.

In areas where minnows are legal, they have to be rated near the top as bait. After all, minnows and other small fish make up a large part of the diet of larger fish. Shiners, darters, sculpin and bullheads are some of the favorites. Some tackle shops keep a supply of live minnows or can supply the traps and seines to catch them. For fishing with live minnows you will need some sort of bucket that can be placed in the water or refilled frequently with fresh water.

Live salamanders are among the best baits for bass. Preserved salmon eggs are great for trout and steelhead.

A good many times you will not know what the best bait will be until you get where you are going to fish. However, a can of worms is mighty good insurance whenever you are fishing for trout, bass or panfish.

57

A spinner might look like a small minnow to a trout. Note the swivel to prevent line twists.

LURES

Lures are nothing more than imitations of the baits we've been discussing. It seems strange that fish will show a liking for bits of metal, wood, plastic, feathers and hair. But the lures, which closely simulate the appearance and action of live food, will often be more effective than the real thing. The five main classifications of lures are flies, spinners, wobblers, plugs and soft plastic baits. Each has seemingly thousands of variations and is made from a wide variety of materials.

A fly is simply a hook with bits of hair, fur, yarn or feathers fastened to it in imitation of insects or minnows. Depending on the manner in which these materials are tied, a fly can be fished on or under the surface.

A spinner is made of metal, with a slightly concave blade that revolves on a shaft as the lure is pulled through the water. The flash of the turning blade is similar to that of a small fish as it swims. Another metal lure is the wobbler, which is shaped something like a spoon and has an erratic action simulating the movement of a wounded small fish.

I've always thought of plugs as lures carved from wood to imitate some kind of bait fish. But now most plugs are made of plastic and designed to float, sink, dive and float, wiggle, crawl, splash or act almost any way that will excite fish. When you shop for a plug that

59

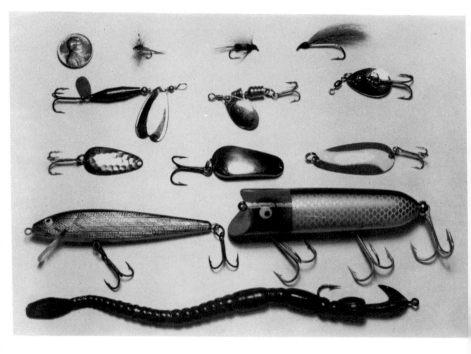

Different types of lures
Top row: a penny, No. 14 dry fly, No. 8 wet fly and No. 4 bucktail
Second row: spinners
Third row: wobblers
Fourth row: plugs
Bottom row: a plastic worm

you have never used, read the description of the action on the box or instruction sheet so that you will know what you're buying and how to fish it.

Soft plastic worms are relatively new, but they're fast becoming the top bass lure in the country. Some float, others sink, and they come in a variety of colors to suit all fishermen—bass, too. Plastic worms are inexpensive and I doubt that you will find a bass fisherman anywhere without several in his tackle box.

We could go into baits and lures to a much greater extent, but it would fill several books if we were to discuss the great many variations in size, pattern and action among each of the major types.

After you've been fishing awhile, you'll probably settle on a few lures which have caught fish for you. Because you will have confidence in these lures, you will become more adroit in using them and thus will learn how to get the most out of them. You will find that nearly every lure can be fished in several different ways. Learn to use a few of them well and you will be catching more fish than the angler who carries 200 different lures in his box. In most cases, the fisherman who has the best catch will have perhaps half a dozen different standbys and will be carrying a dozen of each. Watch for him and try to imitate his method of fishing.

A Tackle Box
for You

I CAN RECALL many fishing trips when my "tackle box" consisted of a packet of hooks, a tube of split-shot and a can of bait, all tucked into the pockets of my Levi's. You don't have to carry a box full of tackle when you go fishing, but you will be limited to using only the gear that you take along.

A tackle box is best suited for fishing from a boat, pier or other position in which you won't be moving around very much. A creel or vest will serve you better when you're wading or walking along the bank. You will have your tackle within easy reach and won't have to go back to the box every time you need something.

Before we consider the tackle that you will want to carry, here's a check list of other articles that should be included in your gear:

62

*This brook trout went for a worm drifted under the overhanging brush.
A canvas creel is handy for carrying bait, tackle and smaller fish.*

When wading a stream, I like a vest with lots of pockets for holding tackle.

Long-nose pliers, for clamping weights and re-
moving hooks
Clippers, for cutting line and clipping tag ends of
knots
Knife, for cutting line, opening split-shot, cleaning
fish
Polaroid glasses, for cutting the glare on water
Net, in case you should catch a fish
Insect repellent, particularly in spring and summer
Life preserver, when fishing in deep or fast water
Flashlight, when fishing at night
Tide table, when fishing in salt water
Band-Aids, just in case.

Terminal tackle in your box should include hooks,
weights, swivels, bobbers, and leader in sizes that will
fit your lures and hold the type of fish you expect to
catch.

As for lures, I'm going to stick my neck out and
suggest a few that have worked for me. I don't know
where you will be fishing or what you will be fishing
for, but here are some which I would take along if I had
little or no advance information.

	Trout, other fresh-water species	Bass	Salt-water
Bait hooks	Sizes 12-6 snelled	Sizes 6-2 Weedless 4-2/0	Sizes 6-5/0 (nickled)
Wobblers	Red & White DarDevle Brass & Silver Wob-L-Rites	Johnson Spoon (weedless)	Hopkins Kastmaster
Spinners	Silver & Brass Mepps Brass Colorado	Shannon Twin Hawaiian Wiggler	None
Plugs	Rebel Minnow Flatfish	Rebel Popper Lucky 13 Bomber	Rebel Minnow Rebel Popper
Flies	Adams dry Cahill wet Bucktail Coachman Muddler Minnow	None	Coho Streamer
Other	Salmon eggs Worms	Lead-head jigs Pork strips Eels Plastic worms	Lead-head jigs

As I've said before, local bait and tackle shops will usually have a supply of the best baits and lures for nearby waters. But in most cases, the fish will be going for one of the basic types suggested here or something similar.

So far, we have talked only about the basics of gear and tackle. Now, let's see how your gear and tackle can be used to catch fish.

Ways to Catch Fish

HERE'S WHERE you start learning to think like a fish. You really can't do that, of course, for you and the fish live in two very different worlds and your brain is much more developed than his—a fact which at times you will refuse to believe. A fish's action really is nothing more than a reaction, a response of his sensory organs to stimuli from within his body or his surroundings. But knowing that, you can try to put yourself in the fish's place as much as possible. The more you learn about the needs of a fish and the various influences governing what he does, the more fish you will catch.

While a fish is basically a creature of reflex action, I've seen so many unexpected and strange things happen in fishing that I'm seldom surprised by anything that one may choose to do. But I would not start a day's fishing by trolling a salmon egg on the surface. Nor would I expect to catch a fish by letting my spinner lie on the bottom. Under natural conditions, a trout will find an egg only lying or rolling on the bottom. An egg moving along near the surface very probably will touch off his built-in warning system. A spinner is designed to be drawn through the water so that the flash of the revolving blade will attract fish.

Choosing a method of fishing goes hand in hand with selecting a lure or bait. A lure must be fished correctly to bring the action that will attract fish. Bait should be offered as much like natural food as possible.

No matter where you are fishing or what you are using to tempt fish to bite, you will be using one of four methods: You will be drifting, trolling, still-fishing or casting and retrieving. Many fishermen become proficient in one of these methods and never try the others.

Let's talk a little about each way of catching fish; then you can choose the one that best suits your circumstances. I know you will learn something from studying each method, whether you ever use it or not.

CASTING AND RETRIEVING

Like the spinning outfit itself, the cast and retrieve method can be used almost anywhere and for all kinds of fish. You cast a lure to or beyond a section of water in which you suppose the fish will be. As the lure

In casting and retrieving a lure, vary the speed of the retrieve and work the lure at different depths to get strikes.

strikes the water, you "feather" the cast by pressing your forefinger to the line as it comes off the spool. You put the reel in gear and the pickup bail in proper position simply by turning the reel handle forward. On the first turn, the bail will close over the face of the spool and engage the line. The rate at which your lure is retrieved is determined, of course, by the speed with which you turn the handle. By working the rod tip as you reel, you can give the lure an irregular motion that will often excite an otherwise indifferent fish.

The longer the cast, the more water will be covered in your retrieve. In most cases, you will be casting while wading or walking along the bank, or from a boat. Try to place each cast so that the retrieve will cover new water that hasn't been fished, until a fish strikes. When you get a strike and have either caught or lost the fish, repeat your cast to the same spot or similar type of water and retrieve in exactly the same manner as before. You obviously did something right, or the fish wouldn't have made a pass at your lure. Whatever it was that attracted that fish will attract others.

It's when you're not getting strikes that changes are in order. You can change lures easily or cast to different types of water, but I've found more often than not that changing the depth at which I'm fishing is the answer. You can change to a lure that's designed to run deeper or closer to the surface than the one you have been using, but the depth of most lures can be controlled by the manner in which they're retrieved. Sometimes you

70

will find success by leaving your pickup bail open and allowing the lure to sink before you start the retrieve. The faster that most lures are retrieved, the closer they will be to the surface.

On a stream, the lure's depth on the retrieve is also affected by the current. On a downstream cast, the retrieve will be near the surface as the lure is forced upward in being pulled against the flow. The farther upstream you cast, the deeper the retrieve. When the water is fast and deep, as it usually is in early spring, I will sometimes cast almost straight upstream and re-trieve just fast enough for the lure to bump bottom as it comes toward me. Fishing close to the bottom of a stream pays off, for that's where fish spend most of their time and find most of their food. But because of rocks and snag you may have to sacrifice a few lures to reach the fish. So rig your terminal tackle in a manner that will save line and gear.

DRIFTING

In drift-fishing, a method which is limited to the moving water of streams and tidal areas, the idea is to let the current carry your lure or bait to the fish in a natural manner. Generally speaking, natural baits will do better than artificial ones.

The bait is cast upstream, far enough above the point where you expect the fish to be so that the morsel will

71

In drift fishing, the bait is cast upstream and allowed to float or drift naturally with the current toward the fish.

Holding the line in your free hand will allow you to better feel the weight bumping along the bottom and detect a gentle bite.

come drifting or bumping along to him in much the same way as his regular food. When the bait is presented properly, it will come to the fish ahead of your terminal tackle and line. As you can imagine, this is an extremely deadly method.

Cast upstream far enough so that the splash of the bait will not alarm the fish. The current will do most of the work, but you must control your line carefully so that the bait will drift naturally and not drag across the current.

After a cast, I usually will leave the pickup bail open and catch the line with my forefinger. This way I can feed or hold line at whatever rate is necessary for the bait to keep drifting naturally. When the bait has drifted through the area where I expect the fish to be, I close the bail and retrieve slowly. A slow retrieve will avoid tearing the bait from the hook and spooking the fish. You will catch more fish on the drift than on the retr eve, but occasionally you will be surprised by a hard smash while you are retrieving. So as long as your bait is in the water, be ready to set the hook.

A spinning outfit with light monofilament line can cast some baits without the need of adding lead weights. Without an added weight, of course, your bait will drift and act more naturally. But in a larger stream or heavy current, it may not get deep enough. Adding a weight will keep your lure down where you want it, and the sinker will bounce along the bottom. Each time it bumps, the line will tighten and you will feel a slight tug. Quite often this will feel similar to the soft pull

73

which comes when a waiting fish takes your bait. Any time you suspect that it may be a fish, strike immediately by lifting the rod sharply.

Use the least amount of weight necessary to get your bait down. No matter how much you use or how skilled you become, however, on most streams you can count on losing a certain amount of terminal rigging on snags and rocks. But you can also count on catching far more fish than you would by not getting near the bottom, which will be more than enough reward for what little tackle you may lose.

Occasionally you may find it more effective to drift a bait such as a grasshopper or cricket near the surface. Use a clear plastic bubble with the bait either on a dropper above the bubble or on a leader below it. The bubble adds weight for casting smaller baits and flies. Watch it closely as it bobs along on the water. When it stops or goes under, strike.

Drifting requires more skill than some of the other methods. Don't expect to become a master drift fisherman overnight, but neither should it take long before you will be joining that elite ten percent who are catching most of the fish.

TROLLING

If you want to cover a large section of water in a small amount of time, trolling is the best bet. At first

74

Always be ready for a bite. In trolling, as in most fishing, getting the bait or lure to the proper depth is very important.

Keep the line tight to the fish. The bending rod and the drag on the reel will tire him.

Once you land a fish, troll over the same spot again as quickly as possible. You may have found a school.

glance, trolling seems simple. Just let out some line behind the boat and your motor will keep the lure or bait working. But, as with other ways of catching fish, successful trolling requires a knowledge of terminal tackle and use of some good old common sense about where the fish might be.

The dry fly and some of the floating plugs are about the only artificial lures not suited for trolling. Minnows are probably the most natural bait for trolling, but just about every other kind of bait I can think of has been used successfully, depending on the type of fish and their basic food. For most trolling, a set of rotating or wobbling metal flasher blades is used about eighteen inches in front of the bait or lure. The flashers will help attract fish. Be sure to use a swivel at each connection of your terminal rigging and a keel in front of the blades so that your line will not be twisted by the motion of bait or flasher blades.

Most of your trolling will be from a boat, of course, but not necessarily one with a motor. Depending on the situation, you might do better by using oars or drifting with the wind.

In most fishing, getting the lure to the proper depth is very important. This is particularly true in trolling. If you don't know what the right depth is, you can start trolling near the surface and go deeper until you find fish. This can be done by decreasing your trolling speed, lengthening your line, adding weights or using lures that dive.

No one can look at a lake or a large expanse of water for the first time and pick out the best spots to fish, unless a cluster of boats in a certain area provides the tipoff. Be careful when you are trolling near other boats; they will often have more line out than you imagine, and there will be a tangle if you cross too closely behind them.

If you see fish working at the surface, of course, you will want to keep your bait or lure close to the top. But don't troll directly over the fish, for the boat very probably will scare them. Determine in which direction they are moving, if any, then try to swing the bait in front of them. Or reel in rapidly and cast to the edge of the activity.

Mornings and evenings the fish are apt to be closer to the surface and usually closer to shore. During the day you are likely to have more success by trolling deeper and farther out.

When you hook a fish, get your line back in the water as quickly as possible and make another pass through the area in which you got the strike, preferably in the same direction as on the first pass. Chances are good that you've hit a school and will be able to take more than one fish from it.

You are likely to do better trolling with another person than by yourself, particularly if you don't know where the fish are when you start. You can fish shallow, for instance, while your partner goes deep with a different kind of bait or lure. When fish are located, you can both fish in the manner that brought the strike.

78

STILL-FISHING

When you're trolling, you're hunting for fish. You're going to them. In still-fishing, you wait for them to come to you in search of food. You will need a lot of patience at times, but at other times the action will be as fast as you want.

Still-fishing is probably the simplest method of all. All you do is cast your bait into the water, prop your rod in a forked stick or other holder if you don't care to hold it yourself, and wait for a bite.

Since you're trying to entice fish with the type of nourishment they normally find resting on the bottom or suspended between there and the surface, most of the time you will do much better with bait than with lures. Almost any form of bait will do—worms, salmon eggs, insects, cheese, canned corn, or fish in chunks or whole. Live minnows are very effective.

Still-fishing is something that can be done in streams, lakes or ocean and from bank, boat, piers, bridges or jetties. I've even seen people still-fishing from automobiles. And it's the most suitable method for fishing through ice in winter.

When you're still-fishing on a stream, try to locate some of the deeper holes or eddies. Also look for a reasonably smooth bottom, so that the bait will be less apt to get lost under rocks or other obstructions.

79

Still fishing is the easiest method of catching fish, but it may take patience. You wait for the fish to come to you.

Use enough weight to hold the bait so that it will not drift with the current. Tie the weight on a leader lighter than the line so that it will break first if the weight is caught on a snag or rock.

While most lures are not suitable for still-fishing, some of the buoyant types can be used effectively by rigging them on a dropper so that they work in the current just above the weight which is on the bottom.

When I'm still-fishing I reel in frequently to check the bait. More often than not, the worm or whatever will be all right. But in waiting patiently for that bite, I want to be sure that my bait hasn't been picked off by a minnow, fouled by weeds or hidden by an obstruction. I don't worry as much when I have rigged up with two or more baits on droppers.

On a lake or pond, look for areas where the water suddenly becomes deeper. Trout, bass and most other fish seem to prefer these areas. A long arm of land that reaches far out into a lake and suddenly drops off is another good bet for still-fishing.

There will be times when you will want to still-fish, but not on the bottom. The fish may be feeding on the surface, the water may be too deep or the bottom may have too many weeds or snags. By attaching a bobber to the line, you will be able to hold the bait at whatever depth you wish. If you're using live bait, you may want to put a small weight between bobber and hook to keep the bait at that depth.

If you're holding the rod and wish to put it down,

81

make it secure. Many a nice outfit has been dragged into the water by some "I didn't know they got that big" fish.

When you're using bait and get a bite, don't rush to set the hook. Let the fish take it until you're sure the hook is in its mouth. How long to wait is a matter of preference and you will decide that for yourself as you gain experience. As a rule, the bigger the bait, the longer the wait.

In this chapter we've discussed the different methods of fishing. This is one of the most important subjects we've covered and one that very much involves terminal rigging. So I hope you will study the rigging diagrams closely and review the methods we've talked about.

Where and What to Fish For

YOU HAVE a good outfit. You know how to cast, how to tie knots and how to rig your baits and lures. You know something about the different ways to catch fish. Now you want to learn where there are fish to be caught.

I will give you some tips that have helped me to find fishing spots, but you will have to do much of the searching on your own, just as I did. I have no way of knowing where you live or what waters are near you.

When I started fishing, a bicycle was my only transportation. It didn't matter to me if the fish were biting in far-off Gitchagoome Swamp. I couldn't get there, anyway. I had to fish close to home where the fishing wasn't so good. But it made a better fisherman of me, for I had to do some hard thinking and work for each

83

Check on nearby waters. Some kind of fishing can usually be found close to home, frequently within the city limits.

fish that was brought home. When you have to work hard for a few fish, you try all the more to look at it from their standpoint. And the more that you do that, the better fisherman you become.

Gather as much local information as you can. Where is the best fishing within your reach? What kind and what size of fish are they? How do you catch them? You should be able to get some of the answers from the man who sold your outfit to you or other sporting goods dealers. Look through newspapers, outdoor magazines and other publications for information about fishing in your area. Write to the fish and game department in your state. Talk to anyone who might possibly know of some fishing nearby. If you know a successful fisherman, try to get as much information from him as you can. But first butter him up good. Your best chance to learn and to catch fish on your first trip is to go with an angler who catches fish. All the more so if he's one of the ten percent who catch ninety percent of the fish.

In approaching this person with thoughts of wangling an invitation to go fishing with him, play it cool and tell the truth. Tell him you've heard that he's the best around and that's why you want to talk to him. Tell him you don't know anything about fishing, but would appreciate any help he can give.

If he starts talking about something which you already know, don't stop him. Pull out a note pad and take a few notes. This will let him know for sure that you think he's an expert. When it appears that he's

"How are they biting?" Watch for fishermen and don't be afraid to ask questions.

ready to close the conversation, thank him profusely for all the information and for taking so much time with you. Mention that if he should ever care to have a fishing partner, you would consider it an honor to go along. Offer to buy the gas, bait and food or row the boat—anything for the opportunity to watch him in action. Even if you were to agree to leave your tackle at home, it would be worth it.

These tactics may work and they may not. It will depend on the person and how willing he is to help someone else. What will work for sure is to get this fisherman in a position where he owes you a favor or wants something from you. If he's a neighbor, help him with his yardwork or some other chore. If he's in business, shop at his store. If he has other hobbies, maybe you can help him there.

Many fishermen are also hunters. If your folks happen to have a cornfield full of pheasants, make sure your fisherman is there on opening day of the hunting season. Greet him every time with "How's fishing?" and part with the reminder that you're available should he ever want a partner. Don't become a pest but don't let him forget, either. You can learn more in one day from this man than you will learn in months of fishing by yourself.

When he finally invites you to go with him, ask what you can bring in the way of food, clothing and other gear. Whatever you do, don't be late. If he says 3 A.M., be there at 2:45.

87

Your best chance to learn is to go fishing with someone who already knows how to catch fish.

No matter how poor the fishing may be or how uncomfortable the weather, don't even think about leaving until he's ready.

Remember, no one gets his limit every time. Your fishing expert is a human being and certainly not infallible. But if you're serious about becoming a fisherman, you want him for a friend.

Different Kinds
of Fish

WHEREVER YOU FIND anglers you will hear talk of game fish and rough fish. The many species that appeal to anglers because of their beauty, wariness, fighting ability, flavor and other desirable qualities are recognized as game fish and protected under regulations such as bag limits and specified angling seasons. Those that are often overabundant and do not give a good performance on either the end of a line or the table are scorned as rough fish, so called because of their coarse scales.

Rough fish are sometimes found in the same water as game fish. They usually reproduce at a much faster rate than game fish and can crowd the others out. But they can also serve as food for game fish and thus improve the quality of angling.

When you're starting out, any kind of fish that you

When it's your first fish, it doesn't matter what kind it is or what size it is—it's the first one and that's all that matters.

catch can provide a learning experience that will be of great help to you later. The basics involved in catching a carp are not that much different from those in catching a bass or trout. And remember, any fish that you might not want to keep can usually be released without harm if you handle it carefully.

We can put game fish in three general classifications: fresh-water, salt-water and anadromous.

Some of the more common fresh-water types are black bass, catfish, crappie, pike, pickerel and trout.

Salt-water fish, as the term implies, are found in the ocean and bays. The number of species that dwell in the sea is so staggering that attempting to count them would be something like trying to count the stars. Suffice it for now to note that the many different kinds caught off the coasts of North America range in size from the small but tasty porgy, flounder, perch and assorted rockfish close to shore to the various billfish and sharks of 150 pounds or more.

Then there are the much sought-after fish that spend part of their lives in fresh water and part in the sea. Among them are the salmon, steelhead trout, striped bass, shad and sturgeon. These fish hatch in streams, go out to the ocean and grow rapidly on a rich diet until they reach maturity, and then return to the natal stream to spawn. They're known as anadromous, a term which comes from the Greeks and means upward (*ana*) running (*dromous*).

Lay that one on your buddy the next time you're talking about fishing.

A ten-pound rainbow trout taken on a three-pound test line. The bait was cheese. All true trout have dark spots on a lighter background.

Trout Fishing

I'VE ALWAYS LIVED in trout country and some of my fondest fishing memories are of a small brushy stream and the feisty rainbows and tasty cutthroats which came from the riffles and shaded pools. If I were to add up all my days of fishing, I'm sure I would find that I've spent more time trying to catch trout than any other kind of fish.

Scientists divide the trout family into two groups, the true trout and the chars. The true trout are the rainbows, browns, cutthroats and goldens. The chars include the eastern brooks, lake trout or mackinaw, dolly varden and arctic char. True trout have dark spots on a lighter body color, while the chars have light spots on a dark background. True trout, other than the brown, spawn in the spring, while the chars and the brown wait until fall.

Mackinaw trout—a four-pounder and a two-pounder—taken on live minnows from a pier. The chars have light spots on a dark background.

The chars prefer cold and pure water in the northern part of the continent, as far from civilization as possible.

Most trout fishing is for rainbows or browns. They adapt more readily to our streams and lakes and to hatchery rearing techniques. The rainbow is generally considered the most spectacular battler on the end of a line, while the brown is regarded as the most wary. Spring and summer are the most popular seasons for trout, but fall offers some excellent fishing with less competition.

If you hope to catch trout in a stream, you must learn to read the water. By that, I mean you must learn the type of water or portion of stream in which trout are most likely to be. If you don't, you will waste a lot of time fishing ''empty'' water. You are most likely to find a trout in a stretch of water that offers him food and shelter. He can swim in very fast water but prefers a moderate current which doesn't sap his energy. In a fast-moving stream, he likes to lie in quieter water behind a rock where he can swing into the current to take food and quickly slip back to his calm shelter. He may venture into shallow water to feed in the evening or after dark, but during the day he will usually be where he has the most cover. In a shallow stream, the deeper pools, overhanging brush and undercut banks are his sanctuary.

Trout streams come in many different varieties, and no one is an expert at reading the water in all of them.

97

But one good rule to remember is that a feeding fish will usually be where he has some protection and where a current is bringing him food with the least amount of effort on his part.

A method that consistently catches trout for me in a small stream is drifting a worm or salmon egg. Using 4- or 6-pound test line, a No. 10 hook and no more split-shot than necessary for casting and putting the bait deep, I let the worm or egg drift into the deep pockets, under the overhanging brush, along the undercut banks and around the larger rocks.

This must be done without alarming the fish and in a way that allows the bait to drift naturally, as if it had dropped into the water on its own. If the water is more than two feet deep, you may need a few split-shot to get the bait close to the bottom. But wherever you can, let the bait drift naturally without any weight. Feed some line out by hand to get the bait under branches and snags. These are favorite hideouts which many fishermen will have avoided. Fishing in a small stream is the best education you can get in catching trout.

The larger the stream, the larger the fish are likely to be. But on the other hand, the more water you have, the more difficult it will be to determine precisely where those lunkers are.

A good method in probing a big stream is to cast and retrieve. Use a spinner or wobbler tied directly to the end of your line. As you work your way downstream,

In a small meadow stream, the larger trout hide beneath the undercut banks. A cautious, quiet approach will pay off.

either walking along the bank or wading in the shallows, study the water carefully. Look for the deep runs, dropoffs, pockets and riffle edges where a trout can find food and shelter. If you happen to see fish feeding at the surface on a bug hatch, change to drifting with a fly and bubble. Otherwise, keep working your lure deeper by casting farther upstream and letting it sink before you start retrieving. If that fails to bring a strike, you might try a flatfish, Rebel minnow or other deep-running lure. Let it swing across the stream as it wiggles and darts close to the bottom.

Keep working downstream until you are confident that you've covered all the water that appears to be suitable for fish. This may be 100 yards or half a mile, depending on the stream. If you catch a fish, stay with the method that paid off. And take close note of each spot or section of water in which you got a strike. Even if you fail to catch anything, you will have accomplished something. You will have learned a good deal about the stream. You will have some idea of where the fish are most likely to be in that stretch, along with the unsuitable water which you will shun on the next trip. If you have covered the water thoroughly, you will know the location of submerged snags or rocks on which you have lost a lure or two.

If you haven't hooked much else on your way down, try fishing upstream and turn to another method. As

100

A shallow riffle that breaks into deeper water is a natural feeding place for trout.

long as you don't see any fish feeding on the surface, keep working the bottom but switch to drifting bait—the "Old Faithful" method. Try worms, salmon eggs, grasshoppers, any bait you have or can find along the stream.

A big stream requires some long casts, so use enough weight to get the bait out to the main current and keep it close to the bottom. If you rig the weight on a dropper of slightly less strength than your line, you will be losing fewer hooks and breaking off less line on those snags.

Quarter upstream on your cast so that the weight will be reaching bottom in front of you and drifting into the pocket where a fish could be. You want the weight to drift naturally along the bottom. If it's too heavy it will hang up frequently. If it's too light, it will not get to the bottom.

Drifting bait along the bottom is probably the most deadly means of catching fish in a stream. This method will work almost any time when fish are not feeding at the surface. It's the preferred way of catching steelhead, the large sea-going rainbow trout of the Northwest.

In spring, aquatic insects may start hatching in the morning or about the middle of the day. As summer comes, the hatches will occur later in the day, toward evening. When you see fish rising to feed on insects flying over the water or floating on it, that's the time for you to switch to flies or to drifting the real insects on or near the surface.

102

Use a clear plastic bubble to provide the necessary weight for casting and to keep the fly or bait on top. If you wish to fish "dry," or on the surface, rig the bubble on the end of the line and attach a dropper for the lure about eighteen inches above the bubble. The dropper should be about eight inches long.

When you rig in this manner, you must adjust your casting to manage the weight which, because of the dropper, is dangling eighteen to twenty inches from the tip of the rod at the beginning of the cast. Bring the rod all the way back and stop. When the bubble stops swinging, bring the rod forward slowly at first and increase the force of your cast just before you release the line.

When you're presenting the fish dry fly or the real thing on the surface, cast upstream and retrieve slowly as the floating lure and bubble swing toward you. Watch the fly very closely. When you see a fish take it, set the hook immediately. The fish will realize instantly that he has grabbed an imitation instead of nourishing food and just as instantly will try to get rid of it.

For fishing a wet fly or streamer just under the surface, use about twenty inches of leader behind the bubble and cast in a normal manner—across the stream, usually. After you have made the cast, close the bail and let the fly and bubble swing across the current. Your streamer or wet fly is supposed to be imitating a small minnow or an insect swimming just under the surface.

Trout are generally thought of as stream fish, but

The trout were taking bugs on the surface. This cutthroat went for a dry fly fished with a plastic bubble.

they are also found in lakes. Largest of all are the lake trout or mackinaw, some of which have exceeded 100 pounds. In most waters, however, a fifteen-pound laker is a big one.

The best way to catch trout in a lake is by trolling. As in a stream, they will be feeding either near the surface or near the bottom, seldom at medium depths. Trolling allows you to cover a lot of water at various depths while searching for the hot spots.

You can troll with spinners, wobblers, plugs and wet flies. By adding weight and letting out more line, you can work the lure deeper. In most cases, fifty to a hundred feet of line will be sufficient. Be sure to use swivels at connections in your terminal tackle to avoid twisting line. To determine the right trolling speed, let out a small amount of line and check the lure's action as you move.

In trolling, flashers and worms probably have taken more trout than any other type of rigging. A set of rotating blades which serve as attractors is followed by about eighteen inches of leader and a worm on a bait hook. The rod tip will dip with each turn of the blades. If it's a steady pull, you're moving too fast. For best results, the tip should be dipping in a rather slow rhythm. Add a keel sinker ahead of the flashers if you want them to go deeper. This setup also works well with plugs and other kinds of bait.

You may find trout scattered over much of the lake, but more often they will be collected in certain areas.

105

Trolling usually will be most successful along rocky shorelines, dropoffs, over springs on the lake bottom and near the mouths of streams.

If you don't have access to a boat, try casting and retrieving or still-fishing. In still-fishing a lake, wait for the trout to come to you as they cruise in search of food. As in trolling, the bait should be near the bottom or the surface rather than at middle depths. Worms or salmon eggs are good baits. So are live minnows in areas where they're legal.

Bass Fishing

TROUT MAY BE the top game fish of cold waters, but bass undeniably are tops in warmer lakes, ponds and sloughs. If you live in one of the southern states, chances are you have more bass than trout near you, but bass can be found in every state except Alaska.

In waters that remain warm throughout the year, bass feed continually on a rich diet and thus grow larger and at a faster rate. In northern areas they're dormant in winter and fail to reach the size of their southern cousins. But wherever you may fish for bass, a two-pounder is a good fish, anything over four pounds is a lunker and a ten-pounder is a whopper.

When you have tangled with a few bass in those sizes, it probably won't bother you that they really aren't bass at all. Black bass, including the largemouth

The bass were in the shallows getting ready to spawn. An eight-pounder and a six-pounder each grabbed a wiggler retrieved fast just under the surface. Such days are rare.

and the smallmouth, actually are the largest members of the sunfish family. Also in this family are crappies, bluegills, Sacramento perch and more than a dozen smaller sunfishes.

My bass fishing started the day I watched a fisherman carefully dock his boat and bring forth four nice largemouth on a stringer. In his tackle box were over 150 different bass lures. And to the obviously impressed youngster who was admiring his catch he explained his method.

"Let the boat drift or have someone row about fifty feet out from the bank," he said. "Cast toward shore, as accurately as you can, into the pockets and near likely looking cover. The bass will be around stumps, snags, weeds, rocky points and under overhanging brush. Keep moving and casting to cover. Try different lures until a fish tries to take one away from you."

I listened to that advice. It took years to accumulate a tackle box full of bass lures and I had loads of fun learning to cast accurately as the boat moved along the edge of the lake. I also caught bass, but not every time, and seldom very large. Occasionally there would be a day or two of red-hot fishing. The bass would hit almost anything and the stringer was filled all too soon.

It's easy to get hooked on this method of casting along the shoreline. You have fun and you catch enough fish to keep you coming back for more. But most of the time you will be casting to an area where there are no fish!

109

When I finally figured that out I came up with some changes in theory on bass behavior. Long ago I became convinced that bass travel in schools and will be in those hangouts close to shore only for brief periods. But instead of cruising around the lake like trout, I learned, they will spend most of their time in deeper water and move to the shallows only to feed or spawn.

Much of the time while you are casting along the shoreline the bass will not be there. They will be out in deep water concentrated in a small area on or near the bottom. Once or twice a day they will move up from the depths and start foraging close to shore.

If you happen to be fishing there when the fish arrive, it will seem as if they have suddenly started hitting after having refused everything you've offered. A short while later you may wonder why they've suddenly stopped. There was no start or stop to the bite. The fish just weren't there when you started fishing. and they left the area before you quit. Except for the brief period that the bass were there, you were only practice casting. That practice, of course, helped you to take more fish when they did come around.

Those rare occasions when the shoreline seems to be loaded with bass will usually occur in spring when they move into the shallows to spawn. During this brief period the fish are in water which you can reach with your lures. At such times the bass will smash surface plugs.

If you hope to catch bass consistently, remember that

When the bass aren't in the shallows, try fishing the deep water where they spend most of their time.

they spend most of their time in deep water. In this sense, a lake which has depths of twelve to thirty feet can be regarded as deep. Few fishermen will work that far down, but they should.

In this deep water a school of bass will cluster in a very restricted area—their sanctuary. Frequently this sanctuary will be along an underwater ridge or reef. From there the school will migrate to shallow water once or twice a day, usually in the morning and again in the evening. The migration route often follows along the ridge, and the bass will stay near the bottom until they reach a depth of eight to ten feet. Then the fish will fan out along the shoreline and move closer to the top.

So, now you know that bass spend most of their time in deeper water. But if you don't care to wait until they come into the shallows or don't have the time, how do you locate their hideout and get to it?

I can tell you a good method of catching bass in deep water, but I can't tell you where to fish on your particular lake. Like streams, each lake has its own characteristics. Only by covering the water over and over, at all depths, will you become familiar with its characteristics. A hydrographic map is a big help, but these are not always available. The shoreline itself will often be indicative of the underwater terrain. Concentrate on the underwater ridges when you find them and keep the migrating school theory in mind.

Now it's time to try bumping the bottom for bass.

Buy an extra spool for your reel and fill it with 15-pound test line. When you hook a bass in deep water or among the weed beds and snags, you must use some muscle to force him from this refuge. A stout line is your best insurance for landing your fish, even a little one.

Early in the morning start fishing the shoreline first. Around the weed beds, try a Johnson silver minnow with a strip of pork rind. Around stumps and branches, use a Hawaiian wiggler. In the pockets and off the points that jut into the lake, give 'em a bomber or some other deep-running plug. When this has put perhaps a couple one-pounders on your stringer and you've been casting for an hour or so without a strike, go down to those underwater ridges.

Anchor the boat quietly in the shallows just off that point of land which indicates an underwater ridge running toward that island. Tie a weedless lead-head jig on the end of your line. Then cover the hook, except for the barb, with the head end of a floating plastic worm in either black or purple. The jig will give you the necessary weight for casting and reaching the bottom. The long end of the plastic worm will float upward from the jig in a slow weave. Make a long cast toward the island and leave the bail open so that line will peel off the spool as the jig and worm sink. If the water is deep enough, it will probably take eight to ten seconds for them to reach the bottom. If they hit bottom right away, the water is too shallow. Try another spot.

113

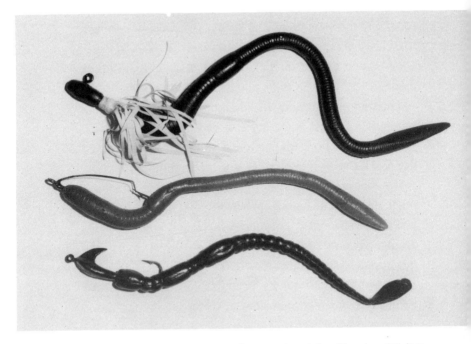

The plastic worm can be used in several ways. A weighted hook or "jig" (top and bottom) can be used without adding weight. With a weedless hook (middle), add weight to the line just in front of the hook.

Assuming that you have cast out past a school of bass, lead the worm along the bottom and back through the school. Gather up all the slack line, then slowly lift the rod until it points straight up. You will feel the jig bumping along the bottom toward you. Now lower the rod and at the same time reel in the slack line, being careful to wrap line tightly on the spool. Wait a couple seconds and do it again. This manipulation of the rod gives the lure a stop-and-go action. Imagine how the worm and jig are crawling along over branches and rocks. And you can feel what is happening as you lift the rod.

You will also feel a difference when a bass grabs the worm. Open the bail immediately so that the fish can take line if he wishes without feeling restraint. Give him several seconds to get all the worm, including the hook in the jig head, into his big mouth. Then close the bail and gingerly gather all the slack until you feel the fish. Now, set that hook—hard! Bring the rod up in a sharp sweep from water level to over your shoulder.

With your drag set fairly tight, gain every inch of line you can to keep that fish from reaching whatever cover he may have in mind. Once you get him in open water and closer to you, do not relax. Let him tire himself against the spring action of the rod, but don't allow him any slack line.

If you have a net, lead him into it as quickly as possible. Otherwise, wait until he is exhausted and grab him firmly by the lower lip. This is supposed to

115

The best way to land a bass is to grab the lower lip and lift him into the boat.
Watch out for the hook.

paralyze him, but he may not know it. So be cautious, lest he set the hook in you.

Once you catch a bass, fish that area carefully and thoroughly. Very probably he has told you of a good school. And when you've located a sanctuary, fish it on every trip, for that's where the bass will be—most of the time.

Panfish for Everyone

A CAN OF WORMS, pole and line, hook and bobber. You're headed for a day's fishing where there's little chance of getting skunked and you'll have a wonderful opportunity to learn more about America's favorite form of fishing—panfishing.

Just about any fish that fits into an average-sized fry pan can be called a panfish, I suppose, but we're talking about a group of fresh-water fishes that ordinarily are too small to be considered as game fish. But they can be lots of fun on light line. And regardless of their size, these fish provide the most hours of fishing throughout the country and are found in all kinds of waters from our largest lakes and streams to our smallest ponds. If your city park has a pond that's not too polluted, chances are good that some kind of panfish live there.

Panfish provide fishing opportunity and fun for everyone. Bobber and worms accounted for this catch from a small pond inside the city limits.

Panfish are not capable of putting up a prolonged battle and are sought largely as food and for fun times.

Among these popular fish are the bluegill, crappie, pumpkin seed, and other members of the sunfish family except for bass, which we've met in another chapter. Let's also include yellow perch and the smaller members of the catfish family, the bullheads.

These warm-water fish are relatively easy to catch and most of them can be taken by the same method, most of the time. Still, let's look at some of them separately.

BLUEGILLS

Bluegills, called bream in the Southeast, prefer warm lakes and ponds with an abundance of weedy areas. They travel in small schools among the weeds and can be found in water from one to twenty feet deep, depending on the time of year and water temperature. In spring they will be in the shallows. As summer comes on and the water warms, they move to greater depths. After the water cools in the fall, bluegills will be found all over the lake, sometimes deep, sometimes shallow.

Use a No. 10 hook and an adjustable red-and-white bobber so that you can try different depths. You may have to add a small split-shot or two about eight inches above the hook to keep the bait from drifting. Favorite bait for all panfish is a worm.

120

You won't find many bluegills this size! These came from a farm pond and the farmer didn't know there were any fish in it.

Whether you are fishing from a boat or the bank, look for pockets of open water among the weed beds. Cast or lower the bobber and bait into the openings, along the edges of the weed beds, and keep close watch on the bobber. If any bluegills are near, you won't have to wait long for action. But if nothing happens, reel in and slide the bobber farther up the line so that the bait will go deeper. When you have dangled the bait from just under the surface to the bottom and still haven't had a bite, try another pocket in the weeds. While bluegills prefer weeds in favor of brush and snags, they also can be found around large rocks and in the shade of boat houses and docks.

CRAPPIE

Crappie, on the other hand, go for the tangled brush and the fallen trees. Many crappie fishermen create their own hot spots by sinking large piles of brush. While bluegills will seldom venture far, crappie will often roam around the lake or pond. This can make it difficult to locate them, particularly after spawning time in spring when the warming water sends them deeper.

The secret to catching crappie is to locate underwater brush heaps at different depths. The fish will be shallow in spring, but down in the deeper brush most of the year. A worm and bobber will get them, but they also will go for small live minnows and small artificial lures.

122

Crappie like to hang around underwater brush and feed on minnows. They are usually big enough to create interest at dinnertime.

You might try a white or yellow jig, or a small spinner with a sliver of pork rind on the hook.

During the hot "dog days" of summer, light a gas lantern and place it on a dock at dusk. The light will usually attract great swarms of insects. Minnows move in to feed on the bugs and that brings the crappie to feed on both.

YELLOW PERCH

Yellow perch prefer slightly cooler water. They are most numerous in large, deep and clear lakes with modest amounts of vegetation. Studies reveal that the largest perch are found in fairly deep water. As with the bluegill and crappie, the exact depth for fishing will depend on the time of year and the water temperature. In spring, before spawning, the perch will be all over the lake at depths of ten to fifty feet. As the water warms, they start a shoreward migration. After spawning in the shallows, they gradually move to deeper and cooler water. More often than not, you will catch yellow perch close to the bottom. They do most of their feeding through the middle of the day, so you won't be catching many at dawn or in the evening. Fishing for them at night is a waste of time.

The chief problem in fishing for yellow perch is to get your bait or lure down to the larger fish, past the

124

A catch of yellow perch taken on worms fished deep, close to the bottom of this shallow lake

little ones nearer the top. When perch are in the shallows, a worm and bobber will get them. But when they're twenty or thirty feet down, small but heavy wobblers or weighted spinners will work best. Or you can use a weight rather than a bobber with your bait. When you find the right depth, mark your line with a piece of tape. This will enable you, once you catch a fish, to return your bait quickly to the right depth. Worms, small minnows and crawdad tails all are good baits.

BULLHEADS

Bullhead catfish, which seldom exceed fourteen inches in length, are bottom dwellers. They like to cruise lazily along the mud bottoms of lakes, ponds and sluggish streams. They have poor eyesight but a very keen sense of smell. Their whiskers, or barbels, are used as feelers for finding food on the bottom. Since they feed by smell, almost any bait with strong odor will do. Everything from chicken innards to soap has been used as bait for bullheads, but the good old worm is still tops.

Since bullheads, like most other fish, become sluggish as the water gets colder, the best time to catch them is from spring to fall. They aren't fussy, so you may as well use 10-pound test line with a double dropper for two hooks about one foot up from a sinker on

A good-sized bullhead comes aboard. He's using a rig with three hooks, each baited with worms. Bullheads bite best after dark.

the end of the line. Their large mouths can handle good-sized gobs of worms on No. 2 or 4 hooks. Start fishing at dark and plan on quitting about midnight. Let the bait rest on the bottom and wait for the fish to find it. When you're unhooking the rather ugly but very tasty bullhead (or any other catfish), keep clear of the needlelike spines in their fins.

Salt-Water Fishing

IF YOU'VE READ along up to now, you should be fairly
ready to go fishing in salt water. In fresh or salt water,
the principles are pretty much the same. When you fish
in the ocean or a bay you will be casting and retrieving,
trolling, drifting or still-fishing. You will be fishing
near the surface or close to the bottom with natural bait
or lures. If you deal with fish over twenty pounds or
need to make extremely long casts, as in surf casting, I
recommend a heavier outfit than you've been using in
streams and lakes. A Garcia Mitchell 402 spinning reel
with 15-pound test line on a 9-foot Fenwick Surfer rod
will handle most salt-water situations. Whatever you
use, always wash the outfit in fresh water afterward.
This precaution will help protect metal parts on the rod
and reel against the rapid rust and corrosion of salt
water.

A salt-water spinning outfit is designed for longer casts, bigger fish, and to resist the corrosion of salt water.

Sailfish and hammerhead sharks: the result of a day's charter boat fishing

I will leave it to the guides and charter boat skippers to tell you about fishing for marlin, sailfish, swordfish, tuna and other hefty types that require offshore boats and a more sophisticated approach. They usually furnish all the equipment, though sometimes you may bring your own. My only advice here is to make sure that fishing is pretty good before you make reservations for a trip. Local newspapers and radio stations near the fishing ports usually carry last-minute reports which can save you from signing up for nothing more than an expensive boat ride. These larger fish move rapidly from one area to another as they follow their shifting food in the offshore currents. They can be around for two or three days, then suddenly disappear.

Now, let's talk about fishing in the surf, bays and inlets. Except during the brief periods when anadromous species are moving through on spawning migrations, the main offering in these waters is a wide variety of tasty bottomfish that will give you a good scrap on light to medium tackle. Among them are the flounder, black sea bass, porgy, sheepshead, weakfish, snapper, grouper, lingcod, surf perch and many others.

You will need sinkers from ½ to 6 ounces, swivels, and hooks from No. 6 to 5/0. It's a good idea, too, to carry braided wire leader in your tackle box. Many of these fish have sharp teeth which can cut monofilament line. Almost any bait will do, though it's best to get advice for a particular area from the local bait and tackle shops or marinas. A good way to determine the

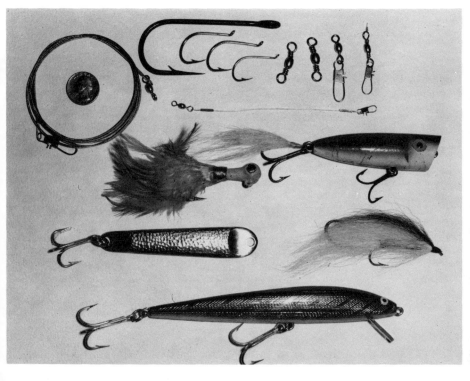

Salt water usually means heavier terminal tackle. Wire leaders, for fish with sharp teeth, are accompanied by nickel-plated hooks and swivels. Lures might include a feather jig, surface plug, casting metal wobbler, large Coho fly or a deep-running plug.

best bait on your own is to tie a weight to the end of your line and use three hooks, each on a twelve-inch dropper, above the weight. The hooks should be separated about eighteen inches. Put a different bait on each hook and settle on the most productive for all three. Try shrimp, cut fish, clams, mussels, squid, sand crabs —even worms if you have nothing else.

Offshore and in the bays, the water level and fish movement are affected by a tide which rises and falls twice every twenty-four hours. The interval between high and low tide is roughly six hours. Best times for fishing usually will be an hour before and after the turn of the tide, at either high or low water. This may not hold true in some areas, however, so always try to gather as much local advice as you can. A tide book, which will be available free at most tackle shops, will be very helpful in determining when fishing will be best.

One of the many intriguing aspects of salt-water fishing is that something really big may drop by for lunch at any time. Occasionally, schools of striped bass, channel bass, bluefish, salmon, tarpon, barracuda or sharks will move close to shore in pursuit of food. You will be able to take these fish, but only if you're ready for them.

Some of your most exciting moments on salt water will come from birdwatching. Whenever you see a group of gulls or terns wheeling and diving to the water, you can be fairly sure that they've found a school of bait fish near the surface. Chances are good, too, that

134

Near the beach you will find a variety of fish to try for. This calico bass went for a live anchovy just off the southern California coast.

the little fish are being chased to the top by the fish you hope to catch.

If you're in a boat, don't rush right into the middle of the action. If the fish you're seeking are indeed under the silvery little ones, which will be flipping out of the water in frantic leaps, they will be spooked by the craft. Try trolling around the edge of the activity or casting into it from as far as you can reach. Plugs, wobblers and bait that can be retrieved will bring some hectic action when fish are in a feeding frenzy.

If you're on the beach or jetty you can only hope that the thrashing fish will swing close enough for you to reach them with a long cast. Be ready.

If you spend much time fishing in salt water, sooner or later you will be jolted by the savage strike of a fish much larger than you had in mind. Most likely, depending on where you're fishing, it will be a shark or one of the rays. Do everything you can to land that fish, or at least get a good look at it. I've seen too many astounded fishermen tighten the drag and break off from the monster without trying.

Sure, you may lose a couple bucks' worth of rigging and line. But you may also end up with the biggest fish of your life, perhaps the largest or most unusual ever caught in that area.

And the memory of that big one that got away will probably be worth more to you than the small ones home in the freezer.

136

Be ready for Mister Big. It took some doing to land this thirty-three-pound striped bass, which hit a surface plug. A fish like this isn't easy to forget.

Steelhead and Salmon

A STEELHEAD is a rainbow trout which, like the Pacific salmon, hatches in West Coast streams from northern California to Alaska. He will spend nearly two years in fresh water (only one year for faster-growing hatchery fish), then migrate out to the ocean and grow rapidly on the rich diet of the sea. Nearly one and a half years later, when it returns to its natal stream to spawn, this fish which entered salt water as an eight-incher will weigh five to eight pounds.

Unlike the salmon, this sea-going trout does not die after spawning. If these big rainbows survive the rigorous spawning process and the perilous trip downstream, they will go back to the ocean for another year before returning to spawn a second time.

Among the five species of Pacific salmon, the favor-

This nineteen-pound coho hit a herring bait trolled fast near the surface off the Washington coast.

ites of anglers are the big chinook and the acrobatic coho, or silver. Thanks to the successful transplants of coho and chinook to the Great Lakes in the Midwest, millions of people are fishing for salmon where they did not exist a few years ago.

The Atlantic salmon, despite its name, is more closely related to trout than salmon and does not die after spawning. The Atlantic is native only to the northeast corners of the United States and Canada. He's considered by many to be the greatest game fish of all and perhaps he is, but many of us here in the Northwest will offer strong argument for the steelhead.

Most of the angling for steelhead is on their upstream spawning migrations, in winter for one race and summer for another. But salmon are sought offshore through the summer and on their journey up coastal streams in the fall. Trolling is the favorite method of offshore angling for salmon as they gather off the river mouths, but this and various other methods will take chinook and coho as they move upstream.

Perhaps the best way to learn how to fish offshore is to take a trip or two on a charter boat. Many fishermen do this at the start, then go after salmon in their own small craft. If you venture out on the ocean or on Lake Michigan on your own, however, be sure that your craft is seaworthy and that you know how to handle it on big water. Wind, fog and unexpected storms have brought tragic ends to fishing trips. Though many thousands of small boats fish off the Pacific Coast without trouble

Chinook salmon usually feed close to the bottom. It's his first one, an eighteen-pounder. Note the life jacket.

every summer, dozens are lost each season, in most cases because of ignorance or carelessness.

In trolling offshore for salmon, your objective is to locate a school feeding on smaller fish and present your lure or bait at the proper depth. Occasionally you will see coho feeding on bait fish at or near the surface, but more often they will be twenty to a hundred feet down. The big chinook will usually be down near the bottom. Most fishermen troll for coho at a faster rate than for chinook. Your best bait, of course, will be the small fish—herring, anchovies, pilchard and others—on which the salmon are feeding. The preferred bait will usually be available, either fresh or frozen, at tackle shops and marinas. But salmon will also go for almost any lure that imitates the bait fish in shape and action.

When the first rains of fall freshen the streams and the salmon enter the river mouths at the start of their spawning journey, you can occasionally enjoy some terrific action in the bays and estuaries by trolling in much the same manner as in the ocean. Coho and chinook will lose the urge to feed as they move upstream to the gravel spawning beds and death, but you can get them to strike by casting or trolling lures.

Nearly all the angling for steelhead, whether with flies in summer or baits and lures in winter, is in streams above tidewater. The big trout do not enter the rivers in large schools like salmon, which may explain why they're seldom found in salt water. And since the steelhead which enter the rivers in December and

Winter steelhead average about eight pounds. This one was taken while drifting an "oakie" close to the bottom of the stream.

January are more plentiful, and easier to catch than the summer-run variety, most of the fishing is in winter. While neither salmon nor steelhead will eat much on their way upstream, the trout does not die after spawning and is generally more willing to take bait while moving up.

Whether you're fishing for salmon or steelhead in streams, keep in mind that they're migrating and are likely to move several miles in a day. The rate of travel will depend on water conditions. When rain brings a rise in water level and temperature, the fish will move rapidly. As the flow slackens and gets colder, they will slow down and may even stop in the deeper holes to wait for another freshet. Fishing will usually be best when the river is dropping and clearing.

In late fall and winter the water is relatively cool and the fish will not be very active. They prefer to hug the bottom while traveling and seldom will move more than a few feet, if that far, to grab a lure or bait. Salmon like the deeper, slow-moving pools for resting spots, while steelhead prefer faster water and will usually be in the riffles or at the tail-end of a pool. Look for them, too, in little pockets where the current runs along a cut bank or ledge, under overhanging brush and around boulders.

Except in summer when the water is low and steelhead will come to a streamer or bucktail fly, you are not likely to catch steelhead or salmon unless you're fishing on or near the bottom. When streams are high and murky, the best method is still-fishing. In the

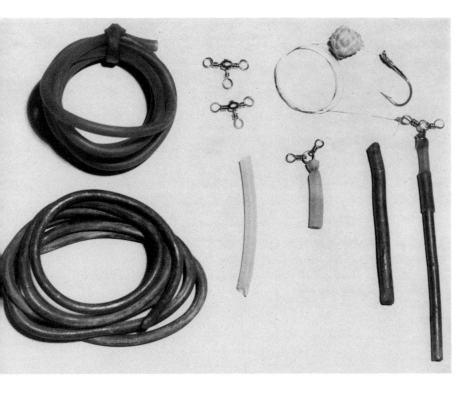

A weight-saving terminal rig favored by steelhead drift fishermen. Pencil lead is inserted in a piece of surgical tubing that is tied to a three-way swivel. The lure pictured is an oakie drifter.

Northwest this is commonly known as plunking. The fish will be traveling then, so let them come to you.

Choose a spot where they are apt to be moving through without having to buck the main current—the quieter water at the edge of the heavy flow, or an eddy. The best bait is a cluster of fresh salmon or steelhead roe no larger than your thumb. Most popular lure among plunkers is the Spin-N-Glo which floats off the bottom and spins in the current. Use enough weight on the dropper so that the bait or lure, which should be at least eighteen inches behind the dropper, will hold just off the bottom and not be carried downstream in the current.

When the water is dropping and clearing, drift-fishing is the way. As in fishing for smaller trout, a bait or lure and a weight to keep it close to the bottom are bounced through a likely-looking short stretch of water.

Many steelhead and salmon fishermen on Pacific Coast streams rig their terminal gear in a weight-saving fashion which will serve you well in drifting for those fish or others. A three-way swivel is used to connect about eighteen inches of lighter leader to the line. A short piece of surgical tubing is fitted over the third branch of the swivel as a holder for a length of pencil-shaped soft lead. This form of lead can be bought at most sporting goods stores in whatever amount you wish. The length used in fishing is determined by the strength of the current. Use no more than is necessary to keep the bait or lure bumping along the bottom.

146

Should the weight become snagged, the rigging can usually be pulled free and you will lose only the weight.

As the streams continue to drop and turn clear, the fish will become wary. Then you should go to lighter terminal tackle and smaller baits. In very low and clear water, you may do better by casting and retrieving wobblers, spinners and deep-running plugs slowly and close to the bottom.

So, depending on the situation, steelhead and salmon can be taken by all four of the basic methods. Offshore, in the bays, and on the larger rivers and lakes, trolling usually will be the best bet. While the fish are moving upstream in high and murky water, be patient and plunk. As the water drops and clears, turn to drift-fishing and then to casting and retrieving.

147

Some Good Things
to Know

I CATCH MY SHARE of fish, but I don't catch them every time I go. I hope you aren't expecting to be successful all the time, either, for there will be days when no one is. I can recall days, too, when others caught fish and I didn't.

If I were to make a list of things to do that would improve my chances of hooking fish, reading this chapter would be on it.

Your chances will be better if you plan the day's fishing before you go. Give thought to the habits of the fish you will be seeking, along with the water conditions you expect to find, and check your tackle. Make sure that you have everything you might need. If you've seen or fished the water before, make a game plan on where to start, what to try first, what to do next, and what to do after that. Don't waste good time out there while wondering what to do next. Know what you are going to do when "next" comes along.

Study the water before you approach. Try to determine the places where fish are most apt to be. Then approach slowly and quietly. Fish don't take kindly to overanxious anglers who make noisy introductions. Start by fishing the water near you first, then the far water.

Concentrate on what you think is happening underwater. Try to imagine the lure and how it must look to a fish. Is it deep enough? Is it being presented in a natural manner? Is it moving too fast for a fish to catch or too slowly to interest him?

When I'm doing a good job of fishing a certain way, without getting action, I start making changes as soon as I'm satisfied that any fish that may be in the area have seen my offering and weren't interested. I may change to a different lure or bait, or go to a different method.

If I'm drifting with bait and have given the fish a good chance at it, I may change to casting and retrieving a wobbler lure. If I'm trolling a plug, I may change to still-fishing with bait on the bottom. Change seems to pay off the most when I make a major shift, not just a switch to a different color of the same lure. The changes are often determined by observing the water and what is going on around me.

There are no absolute rules in fishing, but there are

149

If the fish aren't feeding on the surface, try them close to the bottom. Fish bait or lures slowly in cold water and use light terminal rigging in low, clear water.

some basic points worth remembering.

When you see fish feeding on the surface, fish as close to the top as you can. When you don't, go deep.

When the water is low or extremely clear, terminal gear should be as light and inconspicuous as possible: small baits and lures with long, fine leaders. In high or murky water, you can get by with heavier gear.

When the water is cold, work the lure as slowly as possible. Try to put it as close to the fish as you can, for they are less active in cold water and won't move far. Fish in warm water are more apt to chase a lure, so move it faster.

Watching other fishermen will seldom be a waste of time. Study their methods, then move closer without crowding them and ask how they're doing. If you find someone who is catching fish, admire his catch and ask him how he did it. If you've been observant, you already know how he's been fishing. What you need to know now is the lure that he's been using and how his terminal tackle is rigged.

He may share this, if you've shown consideration in your approach. Avoid disturbing the water or spooking the fish he is trying to catch. Give him all the room he needs to cast and when you've finished watching and talking, don't crowd in on the water he's been fishing. Treat him as you would want to be treated.

Fish can become very smart after several unpleasant encounters with hooks, but seldom will any water be fished out. Pollution can kill all the fish, but it's almost

151

impossible for anglers to do so. The heavier the fishing pressure, of course, the fewer the fish and the harder it is to catch them. Stay away from the easy-to-reach places if you have any choice, for the fish that remain are educated. You'll find it well worth the extra effort to get off the beaten trail where the fish haven't seen many anglers.

The additional cost in time to get there will very probably be more than made up in shorter waits for the bites to come when you get to fishing.

A bite is something alive. It can be just a light tug on your line, or a shoulder-jarring jolt. When it comes, you set the hook by yanking back. The best way to learn the right way to do this is through experience. With bait, a fish will usually nibble until he either removes it or swallows it hook and all. In most cases you will have at least a second or two in which to crank the slack from your line before lifting the rod sharply to set the hook. If the bait is large, give the fish more time to swallow it. If it's small, or a lure, set the hook immediately.

If you're too gentle in setting the hook, you may do nothing more than pull it from the fish's mouth. Set too strongly, and your line or rod may break. You may lose a few fish at first, but only through experience will you find the right timing and touch. Try to think of it as a jab rather than a haymaker or knockout punch. In most cases, short and sharp wrist action will be all that's needed.

When the fish seems to be hooked solidly, let him

152

Let him run and jump if he wishes, unless he heads for the brush on the far bank. Then stop him by tightening the drag

run and jump if he wishes. If you've set the drag on your reel properly, the fish will be able to take line without snapping it. But the friction of the drag and the spring action of your bending rod will cost him dearly in strength on each dash he makes.

Keep your rod up so that it bends with each surge and keeps pressure on the fish. Should he turn and come toward you, reel rapidly to gather the slack in the line. If you allow much slack in the line, the fish has a better chance of throwing the hook.

Try to regain as much line as you can whenever the fish slows or stops, but don't reel if you are unable to gain line or while he is taking it. This will put a terrible twist in the line and is hard on the gears in your reel.

As the fish begins to tire, his runs will shorten and he will offer less and less resistance. When he has only a few feeble moves left or turns on his side, you'll know that he's exhausted and ready to be netted or dragged—steadily but carefully—onto the bank.

Never reel the fish up to the tip of the rod. You want enough line out so that you can keep it tight by holding the rod high while reaching with the other hand to net or grab your prize. Some fish have needlelike spines in their fins or teeth sharp enough to make a nasty wound, so be careful when you grasp them. Also keep in mind that a sudden flop could put the hook into you.

There is no sure way to tell when fishing will be best. Most of the time, though, fish will be doing much of their feeding early in the morning and again in the

Always try to net a fish head first. A sudden dash will put him deep in the bag.

evening. So start early and stay late, if you can. The best time to go fishing, as someone pointed out a long time ago, is whenever you can. For most of us, there are days when the catching isn't so good but never days when the fishing isn't.

Saving for Tomorrow

As you keep on fishing and your catches increase, one day you will return to one of your favorite streams and find that it has been ruined forever by a dam or some form of pollution. Perhaps you will mutter to yourself and go to another stream, only to find the banks which you once had pretty much to yourself now lined with fishermen and littered with garbage.

You will begin to realize that if the enjoyment you've found in angling is to continue for you and all others, you must do all you can to preserve our precious waters and be willing to share them with others.

With the great numbers of people using our lakes and streams for recreation, we can no longer expect to have these waters all to ourselves. The boaters, hikers, campers, skin divers, skiers and anglers all have equal

157

With enough line out, and the rod high behind, you can reach out and grab your prize.

rights to nature's gifts. With any right, however, comes responsibility. And all who use and enjoy these waters must accept the responsibility of preserving them.

Wherever people gather on the same water for different purposes, of course, there will be conflicts. Some of these differences can be resolved only through regulations. One lake may be set aside primarily for fishing, another for boating or swimming.

But no matter what the situation may be, we'll all be happier if we treat others as we would like to be treated. Among fishermen, manners are simply the use of common sense. The first one to a particular hole or spot has first choice of the water. But he doesn't get all of it, and he shouldn't expect to.

If an angler near you hooks a fish, give him room to play it. He will probably not be able to prevent his fish from swimming into your area, so get your line out of his way. He will be more willing to do the same for you when it's your turn. If each of you is stubborn and unwilling to show consideration for the other, each will be less likely to land his fish. But don't try to help him land his fish unless he asks. And when he has landed or lost the fish, the spot where he hooked it should still be his. Don't move in unless he offers it to you. If your lines become tangled, you will know that you are too close.

For too many fishermen, happiness is catching a limit: the maximum number of fish allowed by law for the day. I hope you find that you don't have to take a

To release a fish, hold it gently but firmly around the midsection, without squeezing vital organs, as you remove the hook.

Place him in the water gently and hold him upright until he swims away.

limit to feel that you're a successful fisherman or have an enjoyable trip. I hope you will find more satisfaction in releasing some of your fish than in taking home as many as you can.

To release a fish without harming it, handle it very carefully. Hold it gently but firmly around the midsection, without squeezing vital organs or touching the delicate gills as you remove the hook. If possible, don't touch the fish at all. Just remove the hook with pliers without lifting the fish from the water. If the fish is hooked deeply, chances of survival will be greater if you sacrifice the hook and clip the leader as short as possible. The hook will not prevent the fish from feeding and will eventually rust away. If your fish has put up a hard fight, he may be too exhausted to move on his own. Hold him upright in the water until he is rested enough to swim out of your hand.

Know the bag limits and other regulations for whatever waters you may fish. On some lakes and streams, you will find that the limit is zero. All fish must be released. You have the enjoyment of hooking and playing the fish, along with the knowledge that he will still be around for you and others to catch another day, bigger and stronger yet.

When you intend to keep a fish, kill him swiftly with a hard rap on the back of the head. Never allow your fish to lie in the sun or they will decompose rapidly. Keep them in the coolest, cleanest place you can find. Often it will be better to leave them in the open shade

161

After you catch him, keep him in the coolest place you can find until you are ready to clean him.

than in a container where the air can't reach them. They should be cleaned as soon as possible when you're through fishing.

There are two basic methods of cleaning fish to prepare them for cooking.

On trout or salmon, split the belly open with a knife from the vent forward to the gills. Remove the gills and all the internal organs in the body cavity. Be sure to scrape away the dark bloodlike substance along the backbone. Smaller fish will be ready for the pan at this point, but with larger ones you probably will prefer to remove the head, fins and tail. The bigger fish usually are sliced into steaks or cut into chunks for baking or broiling.

Catfish can also be cleaned in this manner, but you may wish to skin them with pliers. This can be done easily, as indicated in the diagram.

The other method, which works well on bass, pike, walleyes and most warm-water fish, is to slice filets from the bone. Use a sharp knife and follow the steps in the diagram.

It's nice to be able to bring dinner home after an enjoyable day on a stream or lake, but you may not make it home yourself if you become careless while you're fishing. Anytime you are near water, you are just a slip away from a dunking. Always be ready for the unexpected. You may consider yourself to be a good swimmer, but nobody is a good swimmer when he's wearing heavy clothing and hip boots. If you insist on

On trout and salmon, insert a knife point at the vent, with the sharp edge toward the head.

Slit the belly skin from vent to lower jaw.

A little knife work will loosen the gills where they are connected at the top and bottom.

With a firm grip on the gills and a steady pull toward the tail the entrails are removed.

A sheath of tissue covers a dark, bloodlike substance along the backbone. Slit the tissue.

And now the thumbnail can scrape the body cavity clean. Small fish are ready for the pan. Larger fish may need the head and tail removed.

wearing boots or waders, wear a life jacket or some other type of floating device, too. And learn how to remove those boots or waders when you're swimming for your life.

You don't swim? Well, you'd better put this book aside until you learn. Wouldn't it be a shame to drown just when you're finding out how much fun it can be to catch fish?

And as you become thoroughly hooked on fishing in the years to come, don't be sinking the barb in yourself or others. When you're casting, the rod will often dip farther behind you than you realize before it comes forward in a vicious sweep. Now you wouldn't want to sink the hook in another fisherman or a limb of your own and ruin your cast, would you? So always glance behind you before you cast.

One of these days you'll glance back and find some forlorn fisherman standing right behind you. He'll be trying to learn why you're catching fish and he isn't.

The best way to learn how to catch fish is to go fishing as often as you can.

One Last Cast

ON THAT DAY when you're trying to show some hopeful angler why you've been catching fish while he hasn't, you will know a great deal more about fishing than what you've learned from this book. This book certainly doesn't tell you all you need to know about fishing. Nor will you find one that does anywhere else. As we said to start with, you will learn far more about becoming a good fisherman by getting out on a stream or lake on your own than by reading books. There will be good days and bad days, but hopefully you will have learned something on each outing.

In our chats we've barely rippled the surface. I have tried only to help you get on your way to becoming a good fisherman. And I feel that my suggestions on the basics will get you there, on whatever type of water you will be fishing.

DIAGRAM IV SKINNING CATFISH

Between head and back fin, makes first cut across
the back, cutting through the backbone.

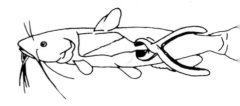

Pull skin toward tail with pliers. One pull should
take care of each side.

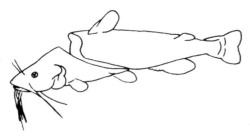

Pull head downward to break the backbone. Then
the head will tear loose, removing the entrails, front
fins and belly flesh.

Cut off the tail and the rest of the fins.

DIAGRAM V   HOW TO FILLET

A sharp, flexible knife is needed to avoid wasting meat. Make the first cut just behind the gills. Slice down to the bone. Then, without removing the blade, turn it and slice along the backbone to the tail.

The first fillet has been cut from the fish. Turn the fish over and repeat the procedure on the other side.

Both fillets are removed and the entrails remain with the carcass.

Next remove the rib section by inserting the blade close to the rib bones and slice off the section containing the bones. Try to take all the bones and little meat.

Remove the skin from each fillet by inserting the blade at the tail. With the skin side down, slice off the meat.

Each fillet is now ready for the pan or the freezer.

DIAGRAM VI   **DRESSING PANFISH**

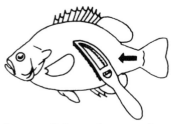

Scrape off the scales toward
the head with a knife or
scraper.

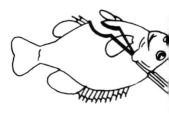

Cut ½ inch deep along
each side of the back and
belly fins for later removal.

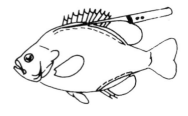

Place the fish on its back
and cut forward from be-
hind the vent.

Cut up to the side fins, then
slice through the entire fish
just behind the side fins, on
an angle toward the back of
the head.

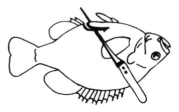

Pull the head upward to
break the backbone. Now
the head will tear loose,
removing entrails and fins.

Cut off the tail and remove
the rest of the fins.

And as you become a good fisherman, I hope that you will be doing whatever you can to preserve those waters and their fish for yourself and all who follow.

So put the book aside for now and start getting your gear together. There are fish to be caught! Try to put yourself in their place as much as you can without getting wet. Put yourself in the place of the guy near you and you'll both have a good time.

Glossary

ANADROMOUS Pertaining to fish that hatch in fresh water, go out to the ocean for a period, then return upstream to spawn.

BACKLASH A tangle of line on a reel caused when the spool is allowed to revolve faster than the line can unwind.

BAIT Any food placed on a hook to entice fish.

BARBEL A fleshy whisker or feeler growing from the corner of the mouth of bottom-feeding fish such as catfish, carp and sturgeon.

BOBBER A small float attached to a line to hold a bait off the bottom and to indicate when a fish bites.

BUTT SECTION The heavier, or handle-end, of a sectional rod.

CASTING Hurling a bait or lure on the end of a line.

174

CHUM   Food placed in the water to attract fish.

CRUSTACEANS   Fish with hard shells, including shrimp, crabs, crayfish.

DORSAL   Top fin of a fish.

DRAG   A device to control the friction of the reel spool so that the line can be pulled off by a fish without breaking.

DRIFTING   Allowing the current to carry a bait or lure along the bottom, or using the current to propel a boat.

DROPPER   A light length of leader used to hang a bait, lure or weight from the main line.

DRUM   Another word for the reel spool; also a species of fish.

DRY FLY   An imitation fly that floats.

FEATHER JIG   A lure with a metal or lead head and a feather body intended to imitate a minnow.

FERRULE   The joint by which two sections of a fishing rod are joined.

FIXED SPOOL   A spinning reel spool which does not revolve and on which the line is removed or returned in coils or spirals.

FLY CASTING   A fishing method in which an artificial fly is cast by the forward thrust of the line, without the pull of any weight other than that of the line.

GAFF   A large hook with long handle which is used to spear fish in landing them.

GUIDES   Rings on a rod through which the line passes.

HANGUP   Terminal rigging hangs on rock, snag, limb or other obstacle.

HOOD A conical metal or plastic covering over the face of one type of spinning reel.

JIG A lure, usually made of brightly-colored feathers and weighted head, which is worked up and down in short strokes to attract fish.

LARVA Wormish or beetlelike form of an insect before it reaches flying stage.

LEADER A strand of thin nylon used as an invisible connection between a heavier line and the bait or lure.

LEVEL-WIND REEL A reel on which the line is wound evenly by a device which moves back and forth as the spool turns.

LURE Any imitation of food to entice fish.

MONOFILAMENT Single-strand nylon line.

NYMPH Underwater larval form of an insect.

PANFISH Any small fish fit for frying pan.

PLUG A plastic or wooden lure which imitates a minnow.

RIGGING Equipment and its arrangement in fishing.

SCHOOL A group of fish of the same species.

SEINE A fishing net with floats around the top edge and weights on the bottom.

SET HOOK To sink the hook deeper and more securely in a fish by lifting the rod sharply, yanking the line.

SHINERS Very small bait fish.

SHOAL Shallow section in a body of water.

176

SINKER A lead weight fastened to the line or leader for casting, carrying a lure deep, or holding bait on or near the bottom.

SNELL A short leader (usually six to twelve inches) tied to a hook, with a loop on the other end.

SPINNING Casting lures or bait with light nylon line and a fixed-spool reel.

SPLIT-SHOT A type of sinker or weight which is a lead BB or buckshot split almost in half so that it can be clamped to line.

SPOOL Reel cylinder on which line is wound.

STILL-FISHING Holding bait in one place, either suspended in water or resting on bottom.

STRIKE The swift grasp of lure or bait by a fish, or to set the hook.

SWIVEL A metal connector used in rigging terminal tackle to permit lures and leader to turn freely.

TACKLE All equipment used in fishing.

TERMINAL TACKLE All leaders, droppers, swivels, sinkers or weights, flashers, lures, baits, hooks or other gear attached to the end of the main line.

TROLLING Towing a lure or bait behind a boat.

WET FLY An artificial fly designed to travel beneath the surface in imitation of a swimming or dead insect.

WOBBLER A lure that wobbles or darts as it is retrieved or trolled.

177

JOHN FABIAN

"I've never been on a fishing trip when I didn't learn something about catching fish." Born in Chico, California, John Fabian grew up in the outdoors, where a fishing rod was never far away. Although known best for his skill with a fly rod, he is considered an expert with any kind of tackle. He has fished extensively for fresh and salt-water species in the United States, Canada and Mexico and has several world records to his credit for fish he has landed. Fishing was the beginning of his occupation. John started a film-making company in Eugene, Oregon, by producing films on fishing. After writing dozens of scripts for films about fishing and having taught his four children and many others how to catch fish, writing a book on this subject was a natural step. When he's not fishing or filming, John enjoys skiing, hunting and scuba diving.

PETE CORNACCHIA

Pete Cornacchia is the outdoors writer for the Eugene *Register Guard*. Pete has been fishing and writing about fishing for over twenty years.